GEO

Ten Mistakes Parents Make With Teenagers

Ten Mistakes Parents Make With Teenagers

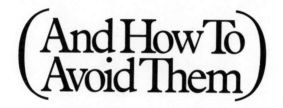

$$\left(\begin{array}{l}\text{And How To}\\\text{Avoid Them}\end{array}\right)$$

Jay Kesler

Wolgemuth & Hyatt, Publishers, Inc.
Brentwood, Tennessee

Unless otherwise noted, all Scripture quotations are from
the King James Version of the Bible.

Wolgemuth & Hyatt, Publishers, Inc.
P.O. Box 1941, Brentwood, Tennessee 37027.

Printed in the United States of America.

Library of Congress Cataloging-in-Publication Data

Kesler, Jay.
    Ten mistakes parents make with teenagers : and how to
    avoid them / Jay Kesler.
       p.   cm.

ISBN 0-943497-17-5 : $14.95
    1. Teenagers — United States — Family relationships.
    2. Child rearing — United States.
    3. Child rearing — Religious aspects — Christianity.
    4. Adolescent psychology — United States.   I. Title.

HQ796.K394   1988   649'.125 — dc19   88-14221

CONTENTS

Acknowledgments /*ix*

Preface /*xi*

Introduction /*1*

1. Warning: Read This Label
   Before Ingesting Contents /*5*

2. Mistake #1: Failure to Be a Consistent Model /*21*
   "Do As I Say, Not As I Do"

3. Mistake #2: Failure to Admit When You Are Wrong /*33*
   "I'm the Adult. I'm Right"

4. Mistake #3: Failure to Give Honest
   Answers to Honest Questions /*41*
   "Because I Said So, That's Why"

5. Mistake #4: Failure to Let Your Teenager
   Develop a Personal Identity /*57*
   "You Want to Be What?"

6. Mistake #5: Failure to Major on the Majors
   and Minor on the Minors /*65*
   "This Room's a Pig Sty"

7. Mistake #6: Failure to Communicate
   Approval and Acceptance /*81*
   "Can't You Do Anything Right?"

8. Mistake #7: Failure to Approve
   Your Teenager's Friends /*97*
   "Where Did You Find Him?"

9. Mistake #8: Failure to Give Your Teenager
the Right to Fail /*107*
"You Did What?"

10. Mistake #9: Failure to Discuss the Uncomfortable /*119*
"Do You Mind If We Talk About Something Else?"

11. Mistake #10: Failure to Take Time /*133*
*"I'm Kind of Busy Right Now.
Could You Come Back Later?"*

End Notes /*141*

ACKNOWLEDGMENTS

To those who have made the subject of family a rewarding and fascinating experience for me.

To Janie, who has practiced what sometimes I've only preached and who should be the one to write the books.

To Laurie, Bruce, and Terri, who were the laboratory and yet never complained. They have made Janie and me look good.

To Tom, Celeste, and Phil, who have brought the grace and strength of their families to the Kesler clan.

And to the challenges of the future—our delights—Wesley Thomas Green, Abby Elaine Green, Bonnie Alice Green, Nicholas John Kesler, Tyler Jay Kesler, and Luke Joseph Collins.

As the Bible says, "our quiver is full," and so are our hearts.

PREFACE

Before you read any further . . .

You see, I was allowed to read this book ahead of time. I know what it says, and I know the man who wrote it. In fact, *he* is the one who asked me to write this preface. (After all these years, and so many books, I thought he'd never ask.)

Actually, I chuckled as I read the manuscript—thinking back on our famous debates downstairs in the hobby shop; the three and a half mile walks down the Illinois Prairie Path . . . and back again; our in-the-fishing-boat discussions; and the countless road trips he took me on when I was a kid.

Sometimes we connected.

Other times we fought.

People often ask me, "What was it like to be Jay Kesler's son?"

Frankly, I don't know. Jay Kesler is the only father I've ever had. Was he a good father?

The Best!

Was he a perfect father?

Not by a long shot. But dad seemed to understand the meaning of words like "process" and "consistency."

And, in spite of his hectic life, my father and I developed hobbies together—woodworking, fishing, gardening. Dad even *decided* to get excited about my canary breeding enterprise in exchange for my *deciding* to enjoy his adult social gatherings . . .

"My, Bruce, how you've grown," they'd say. "Why the last time I saw you was in 1968 and you were such a little tyke."

"Yes, sir," I'd gulp.

I didn't know. Maybe this was some world-renowned evangelist, a congressman, or one of my dad's board members. I could never be too careful. And, we'd made a deal.

Anyway, we found common ground on which to build our relationship. We worked with Dad's less-than-perfect schedule as best we could. Looking back I realize that I actually spent more *intentional* time with my dad than most of my friends.

Now the son is a father himself. I never knew being a dad was so hard. And how much smarter my dad seems now than he did when I was in high school.

One Sunday morning I remember smugly announcing that if I was going to church, I was going in jeans and no tie. Dad (and Mom, from whom he may have gotten his best ideas) watched me get into the family car without saying a word. I thought I had really pulled something off. Now I see. My dad understood the bigger picture. In this book he calls it *Majoring on the Majors*.

That Sunday morning could have forced our family into a tremendous conflict. It didn't. I sat happily on the front row. Dad preached one of his best. (Oh, did I mention that *he* was the pastor?)

I thought I had won. Now, I know *he* did.

Jay Kesler will tell you that there are very few brand new struggles that parents and teenagers face. He's probably right. The conflict may be disguised in a pair of stone-washed jeans or wildly moussed hair, but teenagers are teenagers.

My dad understands that. And he's about to help you understand it, too.

Thanks, Dad.

Bruce Kesler
St. Charles, Illinois
May, 1988

INTRODUCTION

"What are you going to do when you grow up?" I can't count the times I've been asked that question during my years in youth work. Those who ask seem to assume that somehow youth ministry is unworthy of being an adult occupation or is merely a springboard or preparation for "real work" — "the serious stuff" like pastoring or administering some denominational organization or seminary.

For many years my response to this was, "Well, this kind of youth work I do is the kind a pastor, university professor, or administrator is involved in — that is, encouraging and helping young people mature and face adult responsibility."

Fortunately, church youth workers are taken much more seriously today than they were twenty years ago. In fact, the vocation is significantly more sophisticated than many of its secular counterparts. The church is filled with professionals who devote their lives to understanding young people and encouraging them to commit to life-changing behavior. Youth workers, for the most part, are interpreters. They interpret adults to youth and vice versa, helping them understand each other. Thus, if from my years of experience I can help even one parent understand his or her teenager, this book will have been worth the effort.

When I speak to church groups, I often hear parents say, "I really dread the day my kids become teenagers." Or, "I can hardly wait to get through these teenage years." There's a lot of pain behind these words, and they're painful to hear.

1

Adolescence is not something to be dreaded or survived. My wife, Janie, and I have raised our children and are now enjoying our six grandchildren. Yet we would both say that the teenage years were our most enjoyable years of child raising, for it was then we traded portability for compatibility.

When children are young, they are portable. By mere physical effort we can pick up three-year-olds or six-year-olds and move them, change their location. Our size in itself is often a major factor in discipline. When our children become teenagers, we exchange this portability for compatibility. We edge into an adult-to-adult relationship with them, sharing ideas, dreams, opinions, and experiences.

Relating with our children on an intellectual level makes us vulnerable, however, as we begin to learn whether what we did in the early years "took." Do our children respect authority and adult role models? Are they willing to take our word for certain things? The answers to these and similar questions can be threatening. Often we start second-guessing ourselves. Perhaps we realize that we really didn't spend enough time preparing our children for responsibility and independence.

In fact, many books on the subject of teenagers—as you may have already discovered—deal with what you *should* have done when your children were little: "You should have . . ."; "Why didn't you . . . ?"; "You ought to have . . ." But you can't go back. You're stuck where you are with these kids, and you don't know what to do with them.

Do you tackle them in the front yard? Do you square off in the backyard? Do you shout and yell as they roar out of the driveway in your car? Do you chain them to the bed? Do you call the neighbor to help you chain them to the bed? Do you call the juvenile authorities?

I've written this book to help you begin where you are. Don't spend a lot of time looking into the rearview mirror agonizing over things that can't be changed. Instead, concern yourself with learning to be a better parent *now*. Then the teenage years need not be dreaded or feared, but can be enjoyed as a wonderful adventure of growth for both you and your children.

Growth is really what all this is about anyway. So take the first step toward understanding your teenagers by learning who and what you are dealing with. It's called adolescence.

ONE

WARNING: READ THIS LABEL BEFORE INGESTING CONTENTS

Who are these strange creatures inhabiting the rooms that once belonged to your cuddly little boy and your angelic little girl? Why are they always doing such dumb things? Why don't they listen? Are they deaf, dumb, and blind? What happened? How did they get this way and why?

To answer any of these questions, we must first of all realize that adolescents are caught in an in-between world as strange as any world Alice found in the looking glass. Trapped between childhood and adulthood, they belong to neither. But it is even more complicated than that. Though bored with childhood and embarrassed to be associated with it, teenagers are uncertain of the future. Thus they sometimes act like children, even as they try desperately to become adults. It isn't surprising, then, that thirteen, fourteen, fifteen, and sixteen-year-olds tend to do dumb things.

Along with their changing world, teenagers have to contend with changing bodies they don't understand. They are confused about their sexuality, their identity and self-image, and their values. This confusion manifests itself in withdrawal, repressed anger, hostility, low self-esteem, bewilderment, and general frustration. These emotions are then vented on those they love most—their parents and family.

Perhaps the first step in dealing with all of this is to ask a question I have often asked myself: "What does God expect from me as a parent of teenagers?" The Biblical model provides an interesting answer in the life of Jesus.

The description of Jesus' adolescent years is relatively brief. In fact, the span from the time He confronted the elders in the temple at age twelve until He was baptized by John in the Jordan River at age thirty is covered in one sentence: "And Jesus increased in wisdom and stature, and in favour with God and man" (Luke 2:52).

Since Scripture is given for our instruction and edification, I'm convinced the heavenly Parent cited this Biblical model to help us with our own children and to show His understanding of His creation. In it He refers to the four major areas of our lives: the physical (stature), the mental (wisdom), and the social and spiritual (favor with God and man). We know that these areas are all interrelated and that they must work together in balance if we are to be whole persons.

Adolescents are confused about every one of these major areas of life, and modern society only multiplies that confusion.

> Consider the many influences on the young, not the least of which is television. Majoring in the banal, the inane, and the crude, TV glorifies hedonistic materialism as it presents lifestyles featuring immorality and sexual perversion as the norm. Too often the top-rated shows on the major networks present sex as a play thing, values as irrelevant, violence as a way of life, and money as an end in itself. The poor are lured into coveting things beyond their ability to buy, and those who are well-off are invited to splurge their largesse on self-pampering waste. Many children spend six or more hours a day having their minds filled with mental garbage simply because the tube has become an inexpensive tranquilizer and a cheap baby-sitter.[1]

Changing Bodies

Even a casual reading of the daily newspaper reveals the emphasis society places on the physical body. How many pictures do you find of young people who have achieved academic distinction or performed some commendable act compared to the number of sports pages, fashion sections, and celebrity features, not to mention the ads for clothing, beauty aids, and exercise equipment? The priority our culture places on physical beauty and prowess simply adds to the problem of being adolescent in the modern world. Because personal worth is equated with personal appearance, young people live with a low-grade fever of suppressed fear and an accompanying anger.

The physical changes in their own bodies are new, often frightening, and tough to understand. (If adults have difficulty accepting their own bodies and understanding their sexuality — and our culture certainly bears witness that they do — why should we expect it to be easy for young people just emerging from childhood?)

First of all, they're growing at an irregular rate, with the girls maturing two to four times faster than the boys, emotionally and physically. Nothing demonstrates this more dramatically than the pictures of the seventh and eighth graders in the school yearbook. The girls seem almost sophisticated and mature, helped along by the make-up they put on after they've left the house (why they thought the folks wouldn't notice when the school pictures came is anybody's guess!), compared to the boys with their skinny little necks, protruding ears, and Howdy-Doody grins. Most of them look like they'd qualify for "nerd of the year" and seem woefully inadequate to deal with the girls across the page.

Internally, however, these boys are feeling certain urges and interests, which they express clumsily by teasing the girls, hitting them, insulting them, or, in some instances of immature bravado, talking dirty. All this seems childish and disgusting to the girls who are only interested in the ninth- and tenth-grade boys anyway.

The girls aren't secure either, of course. Like kittens in a barnyard who do a figure eight around your legs, leaning all the time, teenage girls need lots of assurance. They need to lean even while they think they're standing on their own.

They dress a certain way and it gets them some attention; so they'll dress more that way the next day. Before long they look like a walking dime store. "You're not going out of the house looking like that," has long been a standard refrain of mothers of teenage girls. But the girls are just experimenting, finding out how others (particularly boys) respond to them, seeking the attention and affection they require.

Adolescent girls spend hours in their rooms trying to imitate images they find in their *Seventeen* magazines — images created by professional photographers and models. The teenager has only her K-Mart styling brush and her Cover Girl make-up kit. Consequently she derives as much frustration as satisfaction from the glossy ads and articles showing beautiful girls who all measure in at about 35/22/34, have successfully survived the orthodontist, and wear the latest fads and fashions perfectly. The magazine girls look coordinated, confident, and comfortable with themselves — everything teenage girls are not.

In today's society beauty is a major key to acceptance and success, and when they don't measure up — as most young girls think they don't or *can't* — teenagers feel insecure and fear the rejection of their peers. Many parents forget what this felt like or, as is often the case with parents who grew up during the sixties, don't understand it at all.

Those who grew up in the sixties recall their own teen years when appearance wasn't important. What mattered was commitment to the spirit of the age — the counterculture. Hair was the order of the day, on stage and on heads. The more unkempt the better; the catchword was "be yourself." (There was plenty of conformity in all of this, too, of course, but that's another matter.)

Today, the teenager who feels herself lacking in physical beauty is not only insecure and fearful, but angry at her parents for not supplying her with the right genetic material or enough money to buy the right clothes. She can even be angry at God for having made her this way. She daydreams for hours in her room, fantasizing about a perfect body, beautiful clothes, and handsome boyfriends.

For adolescent boys, insecurity and anger take another form. If a teenage boy did not have the foresight to have a grandmother who weighed 250 pounds, he probably doesn't have the body to play football. If he didn't pick a grandfather over six feet tall, he probably can't play basketball. Yet a great deal of a boy's acceptance today hinges on his ability to play sports. If he can't, he may end up like Joe.

Joe stayed with us for a while after his dad kicked him out of the house. Well, his dad didn't really kick him out. What he said was, "If you're going to live in this house, this is the way you're going to live. And if you're not, you can leave." So Joe left. (I've found this a fairly effective way to get kids out of the house. Just give them that ultimatum and they'll go. In fact, they're out there on the streets now — thousands of them.) Anyway, this dad called us and said, "Will you take our son in?" Sort of, "We want him out, but not really out; we want him out on you, not out on the street." So Joe came to stay with us.

Now this kid looked like a peach you'd left in the basement for about a year — all beard, like a chrysanthemum gone wild. One morning when we were sitting at breakfast, Joe pulled a hair out of his beard and said, "Does hair scare you?"

"No," I said.

So he pulled out another hair and said, "Do two hairs scare you?"

Once more I said, "No," and then, "Come on, what're you getting at?" "Well, it's interesting," he said. "My dad somehow doesn't know I live behind this hair. I'm the same boy that's always been here, but he doesn't know that . . . he's got some idea that if you raise hair, you're bad. Well, hair's something I can do."

I understood what Joe was trying to say and wished his father could understand as well. You see, Joe wasn't an athlete. Although he was a big kid, six-four, he couldn't walk and chew gum at the same time. But he could grow hair. So he figured it was better to have people say, "There's that kid with the hair," than to be invisible because he couldn't play basketball. Hair gave him identity.

For the adolescent, identity is closely tied to physical ability and appearance. Add to this such problems as obesity and acne — not to mention bulimia and anorexia — and you see the dilemma young people face.

If you were a mouse and could listen in on kids talking to each other at camp or in locker rooms, you'd soon discover that 85 to 90 percent of their conversations somehow relate to sexual adjustment. Some of it has to do with curiosity about the mystery and magic of these strange urges they feel; some is just bravado born of fear and a sense of inadequacy and ignorance.

Despite all the information about sex available today, I'm convinced that our young people understand it little better than we did when we were growing up. They don't know how their bodies work, and they believe the same myths and mis-information that have always been shared from adolescent to adolescent.

Tune in to the popular music videos and you'll be convinced that today's teenagers are highly conscious of their bodies and how their movements affect each other. Some surely are. But most of them are simply expressing feelings, movements, and words that elicit a desired response without really understand-ing how or why.

The frequency with which young people come to youth workers and say, "I don't know how I got pregnant; we only did it once," is about the same as it was thirty to thirty-five years ago. With all the R-rated movies and magazines and books and television available, there are still girls who think they might get pregnant from kissing, petting, or oral sex.

To understand your teenager you simply have to realize that there is no relationship between the apparent sophistica-tion of modern society and their ability to assimilate it, any more than we were able to at their age. And you have to under-stand what a prominent role the physical plays in a young per-son's coming of age.

One of our premier authorities on youth and family, Dr. Bruce Narramore, wisely suggests:

Our teenagers will be relieved and encouraged to know that we struggled with some of the same problems they face. Our frankness can help them form definite guidelines about conduct on a date, instead of ignoring the problem. They will respect us for being open and honest with them and they will be able to gain support and insight from our sharing. On the other hand, they don't want to know all the gory details of how far you went with everybody you dated before you met your spouse! They can hear those stories from their peers. What they want from you is an understanding parent, who is aware of some of the struggles they are facing, and who has made enough progress in resolving them that they can be supportive listeners and, when asked, can offer helpful suggestions.[2]

Finding Independence

The second major crisis in a teenager's life centers around finding independence from the family unit.

Children find comfort, protection, and security in being part of the Kesler clan or the Smith family. Parents know how to buy the tickets, how to get on the bus, how to order in a restaurant, how to take care of you and help you have a good time. Children enjoy, even take pride in, going out with their parents and doing things as a family. When they reach adolescence, however, their viewpoint changes completely, and their attitude could best be described by the old television commercial, "Please, Mother, I'd rather do it myself."

Though it often sounds hostile, this feeling is natural and healthy. It is the beginning of the search for personal identity and independence, and the goal of parenthood is to build independence in the young. Yet most of us are woefully unprepared for this stage of our children's lives. We aren't ready for our role to change. We don't want to feel useless. We want to be needed. And besides this, we fear for them. Perhaps we have not adequately prepared them for coping with the world. We don't want them to be bruised, scraped, and hurt by cause and effect. Thus, the most natural of all processes is often one of the greatest sources of hurt, irritation, pain, and grief in the home.

Again, listen to the experienced observation of Dr. Narramore:

> It is the rare person who moves from the dependency of child-
> hood to the independence of adulthood without passing through
> stretches of troubled water on the way. Sometimes these con-
> flicts are traumatic. An adolescent who believes the only way
> he can find his own identity is to totally reject his parents may
> run away from home, get married very young, rebel against
> parental values, or in some way set up an adversary relation-
> ship with his parents. This is a tragic solution to a teenager's
> conflicting desires between dependency and independency.
> Yet it is one that many teenagers seem forced to take.[3]

As our children grow older we should begin loosening the
screws, not tightening them. Our natural tendency is the latter,
however, especially given the world of information in which we
live. We are bombarded with data about adolescence. Almost
every issue of every magazine and daily newspaper carries
some survey about the rate of teenage pregnancies, venereal
disease, AIDS, alcohol, drugs, and teenage suicide. These statistics are terrifying to parents, but we cannot let them frighten
us into tightening the controls just when we should begin letting up. If we do, we create the kinds of pressures that bring
about explosions within the family.

Remember Mother England? Mother England had many
children, one of the oldest being the U.S.A., then called the
colonies. Mother England had not had a lot of experience with
children, so when the colonies wanted independence, Mother
refused, prompting the American Revolution. As Mother England grew older and wiser, she learned to let her children go
with less and less force. War wasn't the only alternative. She
sent Mountbatten and others to India to help them move into
independence. More recently she's been even more cooperative.

Our children need independence. And we can either help
them in their journey or we can have revolution on our hands.
Either way, independence is achieved. But in one case you have
friendship and helpful participation; in the other case you have
bloodshed.

Christian parents, particularly the conservative evangelical, seem to have difficulty loosening the screws, which is understandable. It is the most natural thing in the world for parents to be fearful about the temptations and problems their children face in today's world; and this, coupled with our desire for our children to follow Christ and live by His principles, adds even more pressure. As a result, Christian parents often panic and overreact. Then the kids overreact, and — poof!

The firstborn syndrome is a perfect example of parental overreaction in early childhood. With their firstborn, many parents go overboard in every area out of fear and ignorance. Thus, firstborns are often the perfectionists of the world; they spend their lives being the mother hen or the resident policeman, keeping others in line and keeping rules. By the time their siblings come along, the parents have learned that children won't break and that they don't have to carry a baby in one arm and Dr. Spock in the other. Children who come along after parents have been "broken in" are more apt to be relaxed personalities.

God has built into His creation some sound basic understanding about child-rearing, and those who follow these instincts and remember their own youth are often better equipped than those who panic at every new Gallup poll and amplify problems with "smother-love."

I'm always appalled when I discover young people whose first truly independent living experience comes when they go away to college or enter the service. For their own good, they should have had many independent experiences prior to this as they were growing up — weekends away from home with friends, weeks away during the summers or holidays with grandparents or relatives in other parts of the country, opportunities to be trusted with time, money, and other responsibilities.

Just for a minute, let's consider the kids' view of "de-parenting." You can expect that your backing off will prompt some insecurity. One mother was telling me that she and her husband had the idea that they would start loosening their rules when their son graduated from high school. Graduation was a major symbolic day: "Now that you've graduated, no more rules. You're on your own." Well, they discovered that the boy began to grow insecure, and that was no big surprise to me.

Generally speaking, teens need to learn to walk toward independence one small step at a time. The best teachers of this are mother wrens. When they start letting their young ones out of the nest, they don't wait until the neighborhood cat is in the yard, then say, "We've had all the theory; now comes the real test," and boot them out. No, the adult birds take the little ones out for small hops away from the nest. They'll jump out onto the branch, then jump back. They'll hop down the branch a ways, then back. They'll venture out to a branch below, then right back up. Then, eventually, they take this big, long leap.

If the first time your son ever gets away from home is when he goes away to college, that's sending him to the neighborhood cat.

It's tough, I know. You give a couple of daughters the keys to the car and send them on a trip to an aunt's house two hundred miles away. But they'll never get to do it unless at some point Dad says, "Eeerghhh . . . well, go! But you be sure to call me at every toll station!"

One of the great advantages of being in a good church is having Christian friends who have children the same age as your own. As the children grow up together, they spend time in each others' homes, experiencing a type of independence — being away from home without mom and dad — in an atmosphere of relative safety. This kind of support is one of the strongest arguments for choosing a church with a good youth group where teenagers can be nurtured in a loving atmosphere by responsible and concerned couples and young adults. Good youth workers do not drive wedges between parents and children. Instead, they help the young grow into independence while encouraging them to respect their own parents' love and good judgment.

Finding a Place

Concurrent with the need to be independent is the need to be accepted by one's peer group. Much of what young people do — much of what frightens parents — is simply an attempt to fit into the current youth culture.

When a father sees his daughter leave the house looking like an unmade bed, he should remember back (depending on his age) to dirty bucks, pink knit ties, black shirts, DA haircuts, tie-dyed shirts, cut-off jeans, or long hair. Appearance holds no deep or permanent significance for adolescents. They simply wear the uniform of the day to gain acceptance.

The truth of this is well-illustrated by a letter I received from a college student: "Jay, it's very hard for me to conform to this nonconformity. Here I am sitting in a library with good chairs and tables all around and all of us are sitting on the floor in sandals. There's snow outdoors and I got my feet cold and wet coming to the library and yet I have a pair of boots in my closet that I'm unable to wear because nobody wears boots around here and no one sits on chairs."

This need to fit in is universal, even during periods of so-called nonconformity. Today, however, conformity is definitely "in," so fads, clothes, and music are all well-defined.

Any Campus Life or Young Life staffer can tell you that most high schools are composed of at least eight to ten different groups. At one end are the druggers, the crows, the burn-outs; then come the jocks and the sosches (party crowd); then the band kids and the political kids; and finally there are the brains, the nerds, and the computer freaks. Young people determine who they're going to be and signal this to others by their appearance, their music, and their attitude. Being a part of or accepted by certain of these groups requires great effort. For instance, the jock has to commit to endless practice hours and expend great physical effort, as well as being endowed by nature with genes that make it possible. A musician or honor-roll student must not only have ability, but must spend hours practicing and studying.

However, a young person can gain immediate acceptance in some groups by simply wearing a brand of sweatshirt or a certain hairstyle. Thus, many kids conform to bizarre standards because they have found other achievements elusive, demanding, or out of their reach. Remember Joe?

(Interestingly, many adults do the same thing by the choice of neighborhood in which they live, the car they drive, the clothes they wear, even the brand of watch they buy. These things give a sense of security, of belonging. So why should we expect our young people to be any different, when fitting in is even more important to them than it is to us?)

Now is the time to make those endless trips to Little League, band practice, basketball camp, and scouts pay valuable dividends. Encourage your young teenagers to follow through on these early interests by joining band, athletics, yearbook or newspaper staffs, drama or chorus, or any other activity that will get them involved with a positive peer group. Most kids who play French horn in the high school band are not going to become members of the Boston Pops or even the local symphony, but they will certainly develop many friendships and find meaningful acceptance. Without this kind of healthy affirmation and encouragement, they may well fall into the cracks or seek identification with those whose only distinction is a mutual rejection of society, which can result in destructive anger because they do not fit in.

The important point for parents to grasp is that the need for acceptance is of major importance in the teen years. Most adults have matured enough to understand that there are certain times in life when one does not need the cheer of the crowd to do right. But when you're young, it's tough, almost impossible, to comprehend this kind of lone stance.

In the larger scheme of things, the label on one's jacket or jeans is relatively unimportant. Brand X is often as good as the brand A designer label. In fact, they were probably manufactured at the same time in the same shop by the same operator. But when you are an adolescent and insecure, labels matter.

Drawing the Line

The fourth area young people struggle with is turning externally imposed standards into internal convictions. I call it "drawing the line."

Every human being has a line of conviction he or she will not cross. This line will ultimately determine individual character and principles. Some people draw the line so far back that it seems there is no behavior unacceptable to them; others draw the line so far up that their deep convictions seem to be worn on their sleeves. But one way or another, everyone has a line.

When our children are small, we draw the line for them. We tell them what is right and wrong; and they obey or disobey, all the while observing whether we operate by those standards ourselves. They also observe kids whose parents have different values, different backgrounds. During adolescence, our children begin to draw this line for themselves. They experiment to find out what it's like to go beyond the line we have drawn for them. They test our values against the values of others.

For example, most parents oppose the use of drugs; but since many of their peers feel drugs are okay and are a way to find acceptance, many teenagers will try them. When they discover they have acted stupidly, or when they read articles on how dangerous drugs are, or when they see their friends spaced out, then they say, "I see what my mom and dad were talking about. My friends were wrong." Establishing the validity of parental patterns is part of growing up.

About 15 percent of the kids I've met through the years will believe you when you say the stove is hot. The other 85 percent have to try it for themselves. Swiss psychologist Paul Tournier makes the point with rare insight.

It is by daring to express his desires, tastes, and opinions, and through feeling that they are respected, that the child becomes aware that he exists, of being a person distinct from other persons. It is a violation of the person of the child to try to direct him in everything according to what his parents think best, without heeding his own preferences. He comes to the point where he no longer knows what his desires, tastes, and opinions are, and an individual without any personal desire, taste, or opinion does not feel that he exists, either. This can be observed in families with high moral or religious pretensions. The parents are so sure they have a monopoly on absolute truth that any other view than their own can only be a grievous error in their eyes. They are so sure of their judgment in all matters, that they impose it on their children—for their own good they think.

This often goes along with the teaching of self-abnegation. While still young the child must learn to forget himself, to disregard his personal desires, to behave in accordance with the requirements of others, seeking always to please them rather than himself. Of course the parents head the list of the "others" who must be pleased and have constant service rendered to them, whereas they themselves scarcely ever bother to gratify any of the child's pleasures which they look upon as mere selfish whims. And they accuse him of selfishness if he manifests any personal aspirations.[4]

When our children experiment, they are not necessarily rebelling against our values. Usually they are just trying to get all the facts, by trial and error, before they draw their line.

This frequently happens with the matter of churchgoing. It is not at all unusual for teenagers to suggest that the church they've grown up in is boring, old-fashioned, or stodgy. This doesn't mean they're rejecting the faith of their fathers and mothers; they just want to explore what others believe and make comparisons.

In the college setting we frequently see young people from creedal churches choose the informal worship setting once they're away from home. In contrast, those who come from an informal church often choose to go to a liturgical church. After a time, many return to the denomination in which they were raised.

While adolescents are experimenting, however, while they're examining the options, parents must cut them some slack and honor this personal search for values and convictions. Decisions made after this kind of testing are often much more valid than those beliefs assumed without question. And parents who allow their children to express themselves, even to be critical of the family, will see less reactionary rebellion than those parents who are always defensive and condemnatory, trying to force their children into a mold.

One of the great principles of parenting comes from Newton's law: for each action there is an equal and opposite reaction. If parents don't react so strongly to everything their teenagers do, then their teenagers won't act out contrary behavior with such enthusiasm.

In her book *Traits of a Healthy Family,* Delores Curran suggests a proper climate for healthy families. The healthy family, she says,

1. communicates and listens
2. affirms and supports one another
3. teaches respect for others
4. develops a sense of trust
5. has a sense of play and humor
6. exhibits a sense of shared responsibility
7. teaches a sense of right and wrong
8. has a strong sense of family in which rituals and traditions abound
9. has a balance of interaction and sharing
10. has a shared religious core
11. respects the privacy of one another
12. values service to others
13. fosters table time and conversation
14. shares leisure time
15. admits to and seeks help with problems.[5]

While you wait for your teenagers to grow up, you can take comfort in the fact that by the time young people reach their mid-twenties, their lines are almost always identical to the lines their parents drew. Even those who do not like certain attributes of their parents find themselves following their parents' patterns.

So perhaps the point is not how can we get our kids to behave as we want them to, but how can we be the kind of parents we ought to be so that when our kids are like us, we'll like what they are!

An Encouraging Word

We live in an instant world—what I call "add water and bake." Television shows us nothing but instant solutions: problem; commercial; crisis; commercial; solution; commercial; move to next program. But life doesn't work that way. Life is a long process.

My mother never took Psychology 101, but she knew instinctively about life, parenting, and something called "stages."

"Oh, he's just going through a stage," she'd say, speaking of some youngster who was being difficult.

What a terrific idea! Whenever they're doing something weird, they're simply going through a stage. And in some strange way it's true.

God is at work in us and in our children, and this six months or this five years is just a stage in the process of life. The Lord loves our children at least as much as we do, and He's at least as smart as we are and has at least as much power. He has as good a memory; He's caring; and He's at work this moment. That adolescent girl won't stay frozen as she is now. The teenage boy's character and values aren't etched in stone.

So take heart. Adolescence is just a stage!

TWO

FAILURE TO BE A CONSISTENT MODEL
"Do As I Say, Not As I Do"

Almost everyone who has worked very long with young people has observed a strange phenomenon that occurs in fragmented homes. These are homes where there is a great deal of fighting and shouting and not much money to spare, often because the father has a severe drinking problem. Typically, the mother is a patient, dutiful, and worn-out woman, hanging on to her emotions and her family by her fingernails. With gritted teeth, she survives. At least once a week the father goes on a drinking binge, usually on payday. After work he will spend several hours in a tavern, then come home and go through a frightening and/or abusive ritual, depending on the effect alcohol has on his personality. His behavior might include sickness, sobbing, hostility, or violence. For as long as the children in this home can remember, the same thing has happened every Friday night—and every Saturday morning.

When Dad wakes up, he immediately knows what happened the night before. He knows he repeated the cycle he has promised to break. He tries to make amends by waiting on his wife hand and foot. He apologizes profusely. "This is never going to happen again," he vows. He goes to each child and asks forgiveness; he might devote a good part of the day to the children's interest, even buying them things they don't need, spending money that is needed for rent, clothing, and household staples—money needed for survival.

21

But there's more to the story: In these consistently troubled homes, sons often grow up extremely loyal to their fathers. (Strangely enough, children do not seem to develop the same loyalties to a drinking mother.)

And there is a strange significance to this predictable loyalty on the part of a son to an irresponsible, drinking father, because there's a contrasting pattern in Christian homes. I'm amazed at the number of teenage boys who are rebellious toward and angry with their church-going, "deacon" fathers.

For years I thought this anger was the sign of a child's denial of the Christian faith; I thought the rebellion showed a fault in the way the Christian faith affects families. But eventually I identified virtues in many problem-drinking families that are absent in many Christian families: these are consistency, and the ability to say "I'm sorry." The young person sees a consistent model of the cyclical nature of wrongdoing/forgiveness, wrongdoing/forgiveness; he knows what to expect on Friday night and on Saturday morning.

Please understand that I use this illustration only to get your attention. I am well aware of the unspeakable pain inflicted in such a home. I'm isolating only two points: that predictability is superior to unpredictability and forgiveness is superior to rigidity. These seemingly small virtues are near the top of my *most important* list. A parent who has these can avoid a lot of pitfalls with young people.

A Model Home

Sometimes people ask me: What one thing can parents do to help teenagers? Above everything else, I say, they can live consistent Christian lives that are predictable and not confusing to young people.

Recently Janie and I visited the Milton Hershey Home in Pennsylvania, a truly outstanding contribution to our culture. Milton Hershey, the founder of the Hershey Candy Company, devoted his fortune, and now the earnings of his sizable foundation, to the support of this school for children from dysfunctional homes, such as single-parent homes, alcoholic homes, and ghetto homes. Children as young as four years old come and stay through their high school years.

On the day of our visit, Janie and I were guests of the administration and toured the facilities. At lunchtime we were visiting the elementary school, so we accepted their invitation to stay and eat with the children. We sat with the students and teachers, in the typical down-size chairs around low, circular tables.

Janie and I sat at different tables, and after lunch we compared notes. We had similar stories to tell. The children at our tables had sat down at their places, folded their hands on their laps, and waited for grace. Then they had taken their napkins from beside their plates, smoothed them on their laps, and waited for the teachers to begin passing the food. As each child was handed a serving dish, he or she said "thank you," took a portion, and passed it on to the next child, who in turn said "thank you," and so on around the table. As we ate, the children had responded to our questions and seemed able to carry on conversation with total strangers—adults.

Janie and I were impressed with what we'd seen because the pattern is so rare these days. Most children we notice in restaurants or even in very good homes don't seem as polite or well-behaved. Yet these were children who, before coming to the Hershey Home, had suffered various forms of physical, emotional, and sexual abuse. At the home itself they were being raised in group homes of ten to twelve children with house parents.

In the time we spent with the Hershey children, we saw absolutely no physical discipline; we heard no teachers yelling. But we did see children receiving a tremendous number of hugs and a great deal of verbal encouragement and affirmation. We also identified a foundation underlying this loving care: consistency. The children knew what to expect and what was expected of them. As a result, they were comfortable and secure in their environment.

If they sense that the environment around them is predictable and consistent, young people will grow up secure, happy, competent, open-faced, and willing to share.

Consistent in Our Commitment to God

Young people desperately need parents who are willing to be consistent to their commitment to God in the midst of what the Scriptures call a "wicked and perverse generation."

When our children were small, I established the tradition of gathering the family around the tree and reading the Christmas story to them. One year I was reading Matthew's account of King Herod's slaughter of the infant boys in Bethlehem when my son, who was only about four or five at the time, asked, "Daddy, why would the king do such an awful thing?"

"Because he knew Jesus was born to be a king," I answered. "He figured he'd better have the soldiers kill all the boy babies so Jesus wouldn't have a chance to grow up and take over his throne."

"Was the king a lot bigger than the soldiers?" my son asked.

"No, he was probably about the same size."

"Do you think the soldiers had babies of their own?"

"Yes, a lot of them probably had babies at home," I answered.

"Well if the king wasn't bigger than them, and if they had children of their own, then why would they obey and kill the babies?"

I said, "Well, that's the way it is with kings and soldiers. When kings tell soldiers to do something, they do it because the king said so."

This time he had an answer. "Daddy, I don't care. That's wrong! A soldier shouldn't do what's wrong even if the king says so. We shouldn't do wrong just because somebody said so."

I remember thinking at the time that my son's argument was precisely the one used by the Allied judges at Nuremberg. To the German soldiers they said, "You were responsible for your behavior as guards and officers in the prison camps at

Auschwitz, Dachau, and Buchenwald; you had a responsibility to a higher authority than civil government, and you should have defied these heinous orders!"

Consistent in Our Respect for the Law of the Land

At this point in our country's history, most of the laws of the land do not conflict with the laws of God, and our children learn from us how to respond to those laws. When I relate the following illustration to service clubs and churches, the room often becomes threateningly quiet.

When my son was in his mid teens, a friend of mine came to visit, a man my children thought of as "very religious" — probably because a conversation with him always wound its way to prophecy or some theological issue. While he was with us, my son and I went for a ride with him. My son noticed that he had a CB radio in his car and asked what it was for. A CB was great for summoning help in an emergency, my friend said; it was also useful for warning other motorists of roadside hazards or bad weather.

As we drove, my boy began to listen to the then-popular language of the CB world. Phrases like "You shake the trees. I'll rake the leaves," which, my friend explained, meant that the first person in a group of vehicles would watch out for the police ahead and the person at the end of the convoy would watch for the police behind.

My son then asked, "What's that thing on the visor you keep fiddling with?" It was a radar detector, of course.

When we got home, my son, who has always had an interest in consistency, said to me, "Dad, what's this all about? I don't understand it. It sounds like that guy is playing cops and robbers. I thought the police were paid to uphold the law and that citizens — especially Christians — are to obey the law. I didn't know it was all a game of not getting caught. Dad, that kind of religion, I don't buy it. I'm sorry, I don't buy it."

We talked about this matter and our visitor for quite a while. I was sure he was a law-abiding person, I said; he was just wanting to push the edges of the law a little bit. I was trying to be loyal to a good friend, but I knew I was defending an inconsistent behavior pattern. I had to admit to my son that I thought this was simply an inconsistency in an otherwise fine life.

My son wasn't all that different from most teenagers. In fact, on the basis of thirty-five years of youth work, I'd say his observations were typical. Teens have a keen sense of right and wrong—even when they're doing something wrong themselves.

"Do As I Say . . ."

Consistency is especially important to teenagers. The "Do as I say, not as I do" approach to parenting simply will not work. Young people cannot tolerate a double standard.

For instance, when the Bible speaks of honoring your father and your mother, it is not referring only to fifteen-year-old sons and forty-year-old fathers. It is also referring to forty-year-old sons and sixty-five-year-old fathers. As young people watch their parents live in obedience to God by respecting their own parents, their country, and their employers, then they have a model for their own lives. In this regard, respect breeds respect.

Respect for authority is not something that can be demanded. It is something we command by our mode of life and our consistent behavior in our children's presence. If we flaunt authority in front of our young people, they will probably follow our example and eventually rebel against our authority.

A timely example of the importance of consistency can be seen in terms of alcohol and marijuana. It's absolutely impossible to make an argument against marijuana stick with a kid if you drink alcohol. When fifty thousand people die each year on the highways in alcohol-related accidents, you cannot drink and tell your kids that they shouldn't smoke pot. It won't work. They see the inconsistency. In fact, kids who want to make an issue of pot will even turn a parent's tobacco habit back on him. "If one thing's bad for your health, the other thing's bad for your health. Two wrongs don't make a right, Dad. One thing can't be right for you and another thing right for me."

No amount of money spent on teens, no amount of effort spent trying to identify with their fashions, fads, and interests, will take the place of parents who live consistent lives before God and before their children.

More Is Caught Than Taught

Usually, children grow up to be like their parents. In a counseling room I occasionally hear a husband say of his wife, or vice versa: "He doesn't love me," or "She doesn't understand me." After a while I realize what has happened. The husband was raised in North Dakota by a German father, a farmer who probably never undressed in front of his wife in his whole life. His idea of romance was to buy his wife a new eggbeater. But the wife was raised by openly affectionate parents; her dad wrote her mother poetry and gave her flowers. So when her husband says, "What does she mean, I don't love her? Aren't I a good provider? I'm faithful to her. I pay my taxes. I milk these cows to give her a comfortable home," it doesn't translate into "I love you."

How do children learn what love, honesty, fidelity, and faith are? By seeing those qualities consistently lived out by their parents. And whatever those parents model, that is what their children will expect from themselves and others in life. Thus, it is vitally important for Christian parents to model respect for others and a giving, generous spirit. Young people who live with parents who show respect for others, regardless of their race, religion, education, or other characteristics, tend to grow up respecting others. Young people who observe their parents willingly giving time, energy, and money to others tend to grow up with a generous spirit.

Generosity versus selfishness is a battle we fight throughout our lives. Young people raised by parents with an accountant's mentality—keeping careful record of privileges and rights, of slights and rewards—will probably spend their lives keeping a tally. Those who learn, by example, to be thankful for little things, who learn to give and share, will live expansive, open, generous lives. Those who are taught to live within the legalistic bounds of selfishness grow smaller and smaller as they grow older. As a wise man once said, "A person wrapped up in himself is a very small package." Children catch the expansiveness or the smallness of life from their parents.

Parents who hypocritically cheat in their business lives, who lie to customers, who do not keep their word, cannot hope to establish patterns of honesty, forthrightness, and truth with their sons or daughters. On the other hand, parents who are scrupulously honest, who do not model life on the edge, provide proper examples.

Integrity and honor are private virtues that are passed on not so much in the big arenas of life but in the small. Does Dad hunt on posted land? Does Mom stop at stop signs when there is no officer around? Does she park in handicapped parking places? Does Dad cut into lines in cafeterias and ticket booths? Parents who ask their teens to be honest and honorable, yet are not willing to follow these patterns themselves, will be unable to inspire these qualities in their children. The kids may not confront the issue; they may even copy the inconsistent behavior. But they'll never respect it. They respect honest consistency, sometimes to a fault.

In many counseling sessions, young people have told me what terrible homes they have. Sometimes I've responded, "I don't believe it; I've been around your family a lot. I've seen your dad in many situations. I know your parents, and I just can't believe your home is as bad as you say."

That's usually not the end of the conversation, however, for they reply, "Yeah, well that's just when you're around. When you're not around, you should see what they do," and they begin to complain about the rather inconsequential and ordinary foibles of their parents. "Dad really gets grouchy sometimes," or "You should see my old man when he's depressed," or "Mom yells at Dad or us kids sometimes when she's in a bad mood."

When I point out that these are, indeed, quite typical and ordinary family characteristics, they'll say, "But he acts like he's perfect when he's in public." Though it may seem unrealistic or even impossible, teenagers expect adults to be totally honest; they expect their public and private behavior to match.

A Good Example

One of the most pointed stories I ever heard came to my attention in one of the Youth for Christ summer camps. For twenty-five summers I just about lived in YFC camps, bouncing around from one to another to see what was going on and how the staff was doing. This particular camp was in Ohio, and after one of the services some kids had come forward to the altar. One young woman was having a difficult time, so the counselors asked me if I would speak to her.

We sat down in the front row of the chapel, and through many tears her heartbreaking story began to unfold. She'd been molested by her own father about three times a week since she was four years old. She'd never told anyone about this and carried a great sense of guilt, as though she were to blame for her father's actions.

As she told me the story, I noticed that both of her wrists were scarred. (If you work with youth today, you see those marks often.) "Tell me about your wrists," I said.

"Well, I tried to kill myself."

"Why didn't you do it?" I asked. Killing yourself is a relatively simple thing if you really want to do it. If it is just a bid for attention, the attempt is usually feeble.

She said, "Well, I got to thinking . . . we have a youth pastor at our church—"

Oh, no, I thought, *now I'm going to hear an ugly story about her getting involved with some youth pastor.* But that wasn't it at all. She said, "He'd just gotten married before he came to our church, and I've been watching him. When he's standing in line in church behind his wife, he squeezes her right in church. They look at each other, and they hug each other right in our church. One day I was standing in the pastor's study, looking out the window, and the youth pastor walked his wife out into the parking lot. Now there was only one car in the parking lot; nobody was around; nobody was looking. And that guy walked all the way around the car and opened the door and let her in. Then he walked all the way around and got in himself. And there was nobody even looking."

That was a nice story, but I couldn't make a connection between that and her problem of incest or attempted suicide. So I asked why this seemed so significant to her. She said, "Well, I just got to thinking that all men must not be like my dad, huh?"

I said, "You're right. All men are not like your father."

"Jay, do you suppose our youth pastor's a Christian?" "Yes," I said, "I think he probably is."

"Well, that's why I came tonight. I want to be a Christian, too."

Why did she want to be a Christian? Because she saw a man being affectionate and respectful to his wife — when he thought nobody was looking. That's the power of a consistent life.

Teaching Moral Responsibility

Gordon McLean has some great insight when he puts forth the following challenge to parents:

The parent wanting to teach moral responsibility to his youngster must begin at what may be a difficult place — his own example. The padded expense account and the fraudulent tax return are real stumbling blocks at this point.

Can a youngster be told he shouldn't smoke by an adult who has a cigarette in his hand? Does "Don't drink, son" mean much when the parents come home half smashed? Adult example really counts here. To encourage moral responsibility:

Be sure your personal integrity is above reproach.

Do not overindulge a child. He will feel no real responsibility for that which costs him nothing.

Don't give a child everything he wants. He will find this an easy step to going out in the community to take anything he wants.

Don't buy off your youngsters. Some parents compensate for their own guilt feelings and supposed failures as parents by giving the child too much.

A father away from his home for long periods because of his business obligations may try to make up his lack of rapport with a youngster by giving him lavish gifts. By trying to solve one problem he is only creating another.

Keep your word. If you tell your youngster that certain consequences will result from his not doing what you expect, hold to what you say. Do your best to keep promises to your children.

Teach a youngster the value of money and material things by having him work for what he wants.

In discussions on rules of the home, the school, or the community, give reasons for the rules.

Moral responsibility includes honesty, justice, fair play, and trust. A young person with a good sense of moral responsibility will show consideration, honesty, and integrity in all he does. In its absence he will show apathy and negligence. In some instances, the lack will lead to dishonesty, malice, and irresponsibility.

With a proper sense of moral responsibility, a young person will no longer be misled into thinking that what is bad is good and what is good is square.[1]

Is There Hope?

"But nobody's perfect!" you may be saying. And you're right. That's what the next chapter is about. In the meantime, how should you react when your teenager picks out an inconsistency in your life? The best thing to do is discuss it. Then if your son or daughter is right, honestly discuss how you can change that behavior and make your life more consistent. Young people will be much more secure with a parent they feel is imperfect but working toward consistency than one who is stubborn and unwilling to admit obvious inconsistencies.

Enter into the adventure of life with your kids. Lead them with consistent examples, not out of an attitude of perfectionism, but out of humility as a Christian who is striving to live a worthwhile life, obedient to God and to society's authority. I think you may be pleasantly surprised if you do.

When young people see parents desiring to please God and joyously living for Him—without using Him as a threatening bogeyman to scare them into good behavior—and when they see parents humbly confessing their faults to a loving God and walking obediently in His presence, their own lives are bound to be affected. It doesn't always happen immediately, but at some point even the most willful young person will say, "Well, if I do decide to be a Christian, then I'll be like my dad because he's not a hypocrite."

THREE

FAILURE TO ADMIT WHEN YOU ARE WRONG

"I'm the Adult. I'm Right."

They say that the only two universal words are *hallelujah* and *Coca-Cola*. (Some might add a third, *Kodak*!) In my travels in over fifty-five countries around the world I've found, however, that there *is* a universal experience: Children everywhere wonder about their navels. They know why they have ears, eyes, noses, and mouths, but their navels baffle them. So, whether it be in the Philippines, China, or Europe, children have decided that the navel is the "done" button. That is, when God made us, He poked His finger in our tummies and said, "You're done!" It is the fingerprint of God, the "done" button— like the Pillsbury doughboy with the little dimple in the middle of his stomach.

We may chuckle at this fanciful idea, but woe to the family who has a parent who feels as if his or her "done" button has been pushed, who doesn't understand that he or she is still under construction. Teenagers have a joke. They say, "Adults are like concrete—all mixed up and permanently set." Unfortunately, sometimes they're right.

Remember the illustration of drinking fathers and their loyal sons? That scenario has a second powerful element; the parent is not only consistent in his behavior, but is willing to admit his wrongs—and ask forgiveness.

For a number of years Bill Gothard has traveled the country holding seminars on family and youth. And while he imparts much useful information in these conferences, the most important point he makes, at least in my opinion, is that we are all "Christians under construction." None of us can be totally consistent; none of us can live perfect lives. Therefore, we must be humble, open, and willing to admit that we are in the process of growing and that we are willing to be perfected by God. "Please be patient with me," says the well-known slogan. "God isn't finished with me yet."

Fear of Losing Control

Often, personality types that find comfort in doctrine and exactitude settle into formulas for theology which afford them great assurance. Once they are so sure of their religious beliefs, they find it difficult to admit that they might be wrong on any other subjects. To admit failure on any level is to weaken themselves. This kind of personality has a domino theory of parenting. They are afraid that if one area falls, then all will be lost. To them, it seems better to stubbornly and tenaciously hang on to error than to expose weakness to others, especially to those who are in their charge.

Parents of sixth and seventh graders frequently come to me, concerned that their child has an overly critical spirit. I usually laugh and tell them the kid is just going through the "Sherlock Holmes" stage. Then I have to explain myself. Up until this age, children are genuinely willing to accept their parents' word on any and all subjects. But when they get into fifth, sixth, and seventh grade, they begin to see that their parents aren't perfect. They walk around and "inspect" their parents, like Sherlock Holmes looking for clues. If you say something happened on Monday and it actually happened on Tuesday, they'll correct you — in public and with glee. If you said something last week that contradicts what you say this week, they'll bring the inconsistency to your attention. If the sign says *stop* and you slowly roll through the intersection, they'll tell you you've broken the law. They'll watch your speedometer and tell you when you're going fifty-six miles an hour. If you told them six months ago that too much ice cream is not good for you and then you eat two bowls of the stuff, they'll tell you about it. They delight in finding flaws in their parents.

The "Sherlock Holmes" stage can be very irritating, to put it mildly, but it does pass. Then the child becomes a teenager and his or her awareness of the parents' imperfections takes on a different form. Teens expect parents to be willing to admit their mistakes and in that way wipe their slate clean and build on a new foundation.

"I'm Human"

I sat with a young man recently who told me about his father, who had been raised as an orphan. When he had children of his own, he didn't seem to know how to handle them. He would alternately ignore them and discipline them in fits of anger. One day after a particularly embarrassing loss of temper, the father put his head in his hands and with desperation in his voice said, "Son, you don't understand. I've never had a father. I have never seen how fathers do it. I feel totally helpless. I don't know how to be a parent. I want to be a good parent but I don't know how. Help me!" The boy took his father in his arms and the two of them wept together. From that point on, this son had the deepest respect for his father.

Here was a man who had had no special training for parenting (as most don't); he didn't even have the example of consistent parents, and yet he was trying his best. "From then on," the son told me, "my dad and I became the closest of friends. I believe I had the greatest dad in all the world because he admitted that parenting was hard for him."

When young people are aware that their parents are fumbling and muddling through, they become open to building a partnership, a kinsmanship that fosters family security. But if a parent insists on putting forth some kind of "knight in shining armor" image with the visor closed up, acting as if he or she has all the answers and never admitting a weakness, the young person (who *will* see the flaws and failures) will feel as if the parent is a person of subterfuge and duplicity. Those teens often feel a need to try to force parents to admit that they don't have the answers and don't know what they are doing.

In homes where the parent is brittle, rigid, unbending, and unwilling to admit fault, the young person can feel obligated to bring the parent to a place of honesty and humility. They can unknowingly erode the parent's authority, like water dripping on a rock, relentlessly, unceasingly, until the inflexible, never-admit-wrong parent is brought to his or her knees. They may spend their teenage years scheming, setting traps and snares, trying to catch the parent and force him or her to admit humanity.

The Value of "Forgive Me"

Young people are as individual as snowflakes, but they are nowhere near as fragile. In fact, there are as many parenting styles as there are parents; there are many good ways to raise a good family. But the mistakes a family cannot recover from are arrogance, inflexibility, uptightness, stubbornness, and the inability to say "I am wrong" and seek forgiveness.

Parents don't need to be perfect; they need to be honest and humble. The three most difficult sentences for parents to say need to be said. They are short, but I'll not deny that they don't come out easily: "I'm sorry. I was wrong. Please forgive me."

Generally speaking, teenagers who have not heard a parent say these sentences will never learn how to speak them. They, too, will stubbornly, rigidly hang on to their own positions and a negative cycle will pass on to a new generation. Young people who have learned, by example, to back off, admit mistakes, and start over again live happier lives than those who have had only this "I am always right" attitude modeled for them.

Of course there will be plenty of times when parents need to be the ones doing the forgiving; but they should not always be the ones taking the benevolent position of forgiver. There is always a certain element of superiority and power in forgiving. When a parent gives up that power, takes on humility, and is willing to say, "I was wrong. I'm sorry. Please forgive me," then the young person can learn two lessons at once: He or she can see that it's okay to admit imperfection and can also experience what it's like to forgive. It is precisely this ability to accept imperfection and forgive that builds loyalty into many other- wise difficult, problem-drinking homes. Obviously, I'm not ad- vocating that anyone become a problem drinker. I'm simply pointing out the power of the words "I'm sorry. Please forgive me. I was wrong."

This simple Biblical principle of forgiveness — of forgiving and being forgiven — is at the root of successful parenting. But it is not simply a tool for a smoother family life; it is an example of God's forgiving nature toward us and His desire that we be the kind of people who seek His forgiveness. As we model, this humility and this willingness to admit failure will teach deep theological lessons that will make our children's faith stronger throughout the rest of their lives.

David Seamands understands this when he says,

> Many years ago I was driven to the conclusion that the two major causes of most emotional problems among evangelical Christians are these: the failure to understand, receive, and live out God's unconditional grace and forgiveness; and the failure to give out that unconditional love, forgiveness, and grace to other people. . . . We read, we hear, we believe a good theology of grace. But that's not the way we live. We be- lieve grace in our heads but not in our gut level feelings or in our relationships. . . . But it's all on a head level. The good news of the Gospel of grace has not penetrated the level of our emotions.[1]

An apology to a son or daughter might be most effective if it includes a reason why such a negative behavior surfaced. For example, let's say I lost my temper last night when my son came home a half-hour after our agreed time. Over breakfast I might apologize and explain, "Son, I lost my temper, shouted, and said some very unfair, exaggerated things last night and I want you to understand why. I was very frightened. You came home after you said you would be in. It's not so much that 11:30 P.M. is a magical hour and that you're a bad person if you come in at midnight. The problem is that during that half-hour I kept wondering why you weren't home. I kept seeing you splattered all over the street somewhere, or the car rolled over in a ditch someplace — and you being taken in an emergency helicopter to the hospital. I had visions of your organs being transplanted into someone else, and it simply terrified me.

"Then when you walked in the house and seemed so glib and unconcerned about it all, I felt as if you had flouted my love and concern. I was worried sick and you were happy as a goose, and that made me angry. Then I blew it. I yelled at you to try and make you understand how badly I felt. When I do that, I feel embarrassed and ashamed. I could hardly sleep because of it. Please forgive me for shouting at you; I was wrong."

As a teenager I had a friend who was so terrified of being beaten by his father that he would vomit every time he was still out with us at 11:30. I'm ashamed to have to admit that we sometimes would fool him for effect. We would say "Ralph, it's 11:30" when we were a half-hour or an hour from home, and he'd immediately begin to vomit.

If a parent always disciplines from a position of power ("I guess I told him. Next time he'll come in at 11:30; he won't dare be late"), only a small part of the intended purpose of the discipline will be achieved. He may maintain order, but he won't accomplish much else. He may instill a gut-wrenching fear in his son, but he won't build a loving respect for authority nor instill a sense of responsibility. And inevitably that fear will turn into rebellion in some form.

The Other Side of the Coin

Of course, parents aren't always wrong, and knowing how to be right with the correct attitude is also important. The finest treatment of loving confrontation I've ever come across is in

David Augsburger's book *Caring Enough to Confront.* Here's a summary of the "basic alternatives open in most conflict situations."

1. "I'll get him" is the I-win-you-lose-because-I'm-right-you're-wrong position in conflict. From this viewpoint, the attitude toward conflict is that the issues are all quite clear — and simple. Someone is right — totally right, and someone is wrong — completely wrong. Fortunately, I'm right (as usual) and you're wrong. Except, in this case, it could prove to be someone else besides or instead of the truth — on my side. It's my duty to put you right. This "win-lose" stance uses all power and little or no love. Goal is valued above relationship. "My way is the only way," the person feels.

2. "I'll get out" is the I'm-uncomfortable-so-I'll-withdraw stance toward conflict. The viewpoint here is that conflicts are hopeless, people cannot be changed; we either overlook them or withdraw. Conflicts are to be avoided at all costs. When they threaten, get out of their way.

Withdrawal has its advantages if instant safety is the all-important thing. But it is a way out of conflict, not a way through. And a way out is no way at all.

In this lose-lose stance everyone loses. There is no risk of power, no trusting love. "Show me the nearest exit," the person requests over the shoulder. It's a no-way or any way response of flight.

3. "I'll give in" is the I'll yield-to-be-nice-since-I-need-your-friendship approach. This perspective on conflict says that differences are disastrous. If they come out into the open, anything can happen. Anything evil, that is. It's far better to be nice, to submit, to go along with the other's demands and stay friends.

Yielding to keep contact will serve you well in many situations. But as a rule, it falls short. You become a doormat. A nice guy or gal. Frustrated. Yet smiling. The more tense and tight on the inside, the more generous and submissive on the outside.

4. "I'll meet you halfway" is the I-have-only-half-the-truth-and-I-need-your-half position. The attitude is one of creative compromise. Conflict is natural, and everyone should be willing to come part way in an attempt to resolve things. A willingness to give a little will lead to a working solution which is satisfactory to everyone.

Compromise is a gift to human relationships. We move forward on the basis of thoughtful, careful consensus and compromise in most decisions in conflict. But it calls for at least a partial sacrifice of deeply held views and goals which may cost all of us the loss of the best to reach the good of agreement.

When we begin with a decision to compromise, we run the risk that my half of the truth added to your half may not give us the whole truth and nothing but the truth. We may have two half-truths. Or the combination may produce a whole untruth. Only when we care enough to tussle with truth can we test, retest, refine and perhaps find more of it through our working at it seriously.

5. "I care enough to confront" is the I-want-relationship-and-I-also-want-honest-integrity position. Conflict is viewed as neutral (neither good nor bad) and natural (neither to be avoided nor short-circuited). Working through differences by giving clear messages of "I care" and "I want," which both care and confront, is most helpful.

This is interpersonal communication at its best. Caring—I want to stay in respectful relationships with you, *and* confronting—I want you to know where I stand and what I'm feeling, needing, valuing and wanting.[2]

Ultimately, Augsburger is recommending honesty as the best policy in conflict resolution, as I've recommended honesty in acknowledging our humanity. It takes courage, but, again, I urge you to try it. The scowling, overly critical young people in your house may ease their attack.

FAILURE TO GIVE HONEST ANSWERS TO HONEST QUESTIONS

"Because I Said So, That's Why"

"Because when I say frog, that means jump. And when I say jump, you say how high."

"Because I'm bigger than you, that's why."

"Because you live in my house and I pay all the bills. And as long as you're living under my roof, you'll do as I say. When you're big enough to have you own house and live under your own roof, then you can make the rules. In the meantime, I'm going to make the rules and you're going to do as I say. Exactly as I say. Have you got that straight?"

Do any of these responses have a familiar ring? I'm sure they do, for I've met many parents who think this is the way you answer teenagers who ask "Why?"

Now that approach may work with a ten-year-old who is two feet shorter and a hundred pounds lighter than you. But kids grow up fast, and before long this dictatorial stance fails to bring the desired result. And, of course, even with small children appearances are deceiving; the power wielded by this heavy-handed method is really an illusion. Remember the story of the teacher who said, "Johnny sit down"? Johnny stood up. She said, "Johnny sit down." Johnny stood up. Finally, she walked over and sat Johnny down. He stayed there, but he quipped, "I'm sitting on the outside, but I'm standing on the inside."

When we can't or won't give logical answers to their "why?" questions, young people often withdraw and harbor deep resentment against us. Then their frustration develops into full-scale rebellion: "You just wait till I get out of this house; then I'm going to do as I please. Just as soon as I'm able to get on my own, I'm going to do all the things they say I can't."

One of my best friends in high school used to mumble similar words as we walked to school. "You wait till I'm eighteen; I'm going to leave this house. I'm going to get out and do just what I want to do, and my old man's not going to have a thing to say about it."

I used to try to reason with him. Sometimes I'd disagree and argue with him; other times I'd try to get him to see things more clearly, try to keep him from doing something stupid that would ruin his life. But in general I really didn't take his threats too seriously; I thought he was just blowing off steam when he got mad at his father, as many kids do. However, eventually my friend did exactly what he'd said he'd do. At eighteen, he announced his independence and began doing all the things his dad had frowned upon. He got himself into all sorts of trouble. His dad's authoritarian, unreasonable approach to parenting became a self-fulfilling prophecy, plunging my friend into a negative lifestyle that almost destroyed him.

Sound Mind

When teaching an animal to behave, we don't have to worry about "why?" questions. We simply set up an electric fence that gives a shock every time the animal goes out of bounds. It doesn't take the animal long to learn the lesson: Don't touch.

But people are different from animals. God has created them with sound minds and the ability to think and reason. President Lyndon Johnson was fond of quoting Isaiah 1:18: "Come now, and let us reason together, saith the Lord." He believed that two people could sit down together, discuss their differences, and come to some reasonable conclusions. This reasoning together is a God-given ability.

As our children move into their teenage years, this reason starts to replace portability. Then we can begin to teach not only proper behavior, but why the proper behavior is important. In fact, in the college setting where I'm now working, I often tell the students: those who know *how* to do things will always have a job. But those who know *why* they are doing things will always be their bosses. And those who know the Author of the How and Why, those who do their work for God out of love and obedience, will not only have a job and be the bosses, but will find fulfillment in what they are doing.

But the *how,* the *why,* and the *who* have to fit together, so an important part of parenting is helping your children understand the compelling logic and reason behind your expectations. To neglect or refuse to do so is a tragic error.

When our kids were little, one of our house rules was, "You can't ride your bike in the street." Did they ever complain? You bet they did. I can't count the times we heard, "We're the only kids in the whole world who can't ride our bikes in the street."

"Just think what individuals you are," I'd joke. "You're the only kids in the *whole* world who can't ride your bikes in the street." But they didn't think it was funny.

However, one night at supper our daughter Terri, who was quite small at the time, said, "Daddy! Timmy got crunched by a car today."

"What!" I said.

Then she told me the neighbor kid, Timmy, was three streets away from home when he got hit, "crunched," by a car.

I said, "Now do you understand why Daddy doesn't want you riding your bike in the street?"

"You don't want us to be crunched by a car?"

"Yeah, that's it," I said. "We don't want you crunched because we love you."

As young as she was, Terri was beginning to learn the important *why* behind one of our house rules.

Conflicting Voices

When I've made this point in a speech, I've sometimes had fathers in the audience say to me, "Well, Jay, I don't agree. When I was a boy, my dad said something and I did it. I didn't sass back and I didn't ask why. I knew you should do certain things because adults said so. In those days we trusted adults and did what they told us to do." I agree that there was a period in history when this was true in most households. Children did obey their parents without question; sometimes out of fear, but often because they trusted their parents. They knew their parents held to certain principles of virtue, honor, fidelity, and loyalty that were accepted by the majority of people in the culture in that day.

But life now, in this last quarter of the twentieth century, is much more complicated. Teens are barraged with voices from their peers, from television, from celebrity role models, from the lyrics of rock music, from the many in our culture who openly voice their opinions and promote their deviant life-styles.

Because of this, many educators have attempted to move young people away from the "do as I do because I'm an adult" model. Their objective is to help teenagers develop discriminating minds so they'll be able to deal with confusing, and often contradictory, data.

A generation ago, many young people were considered conscientious students because they could take accurate notes from a teacher's lecture or blackboard work, study those notes, and then repeat the information on a test paper. Today, however, our young people are faced with an explosion of information. No one can possibly store it all. In fact, we use electronic equipment and gadgetry to do much of that storage and retrieval of factual information. Our young people have immense amounts of information at their fingertips. They don't need more information; what they need is discrimination. They need to be able to distinguish between bad and good information and make proper judgments about its use.

Twenty-five years ago if you asked a teacher, "Who's your best student?" she might have said, "Peter's my best student; he always gives the right answers." If you asked that same question today, the teacher would probably reply, "Peter's my best student; he asks the best questions."

This change in the approach to learning has occurred in one or two generations, and it is behind a lot of confusion parents face as they deal with their children. When a teenager questions us, it's usually not because he or she wants to be sassy or question our authority or be disobedient. Teens simply want to know where we got our information and why we believe what we believe and why we want them to do certain things.

In a simpler time, people trusted general sources of information: "I saw it in the paper"; "I heard it on the news." But what we now read in our papers, or see and hear on the evening news, might not be true at all. We know that individuals, even governments, have found it pragmatic to tell repeated lies to us to *disinform* us! Don't you feel deceived when you learn that something you have believed in — argued with your barber about for years — is actually a lie put forth to accomplish some political purpose? Each month it seems that a new Senate investigation has uncovered another deception. You can no longer tell the good guys by their white hats.

Is it any wonder our children demand answers? Is it surprising that they want to know the reasons behind what is expected of them? They simply want to learn how to make their own discerning judgments.

When I was at Youth for Christ, we spent more money than I want to admit to hire Michigan State University to do a survey on the subject of young people and authority: "To whom do young people go when they want an answer to a question?" To no one's surprise, the survey indicated that the most influential force in an adolescent's life is the peer group. The great surprise was that parents came next in importance; in fact, they were within tenths of a point of peers. No one anticipated this finding: Teens want answers from their parents.

That's Not Good Enough

"Why do I have to do this?" When the question comes, you had better know the answer. I learned this the hard way with my own kids when I couldn't give good reasons for a number of the rules in our house. "Well, because the women at the church would frown on that." Or, "They don't expect the pastor's son to do that." At one point, Janie and I sat down and made a decision; we were not going to be pressured into raising our family on the basis of what the women of the church would think. Our kids deserved as much grace as any of the other church kids.

One day after I'd spoken about this at a Rotary Club luncheon, a man came up to me and, without a word, pulled out his billfold and laid down pictures of five boys, side by side. Then he laid down another picture. He was crying the whole time he did this, and finally said, "Jay, I'm going to tell you something. I prided myself on running a tight ship. I prided myself that I was in charge. And now all five of these boys have left home, and not one of them will talk to me. None of them have even been home for Christmas for two years." He was sobbing by this time, almost beyond control.

Then he said, pointing to the one picture set off by itself, "But, Jay, this boy is still at home. I don't care what they say; I'm not going to have this boy leave. And I'm not going to do the same with him."

He'd slipped an odd phrase in there, and I said, "What do you mean *they say*?"

"Well, I've given it a lot of thought and some prayer, and I think the reason those boys are gone is because I was trying to please somebody else. . . . I was trying to please my father. He was one of those tough dads, and I was afraid he would think I was soft on my kids. So I came down hard on my boys. If my dad did it once, I did it twice. I was going to be better than he was at it. But I've just managed to drive my boys away."

When this father analyzed his own reasons for his rules or for the way he enforced them he found them wanting. As a reason, "What will 'they' say?" doesn't hold water.

Educating Young Minds

In the context of my work as an administrator of an evangelical Christian college, people often ask, "Why don't you simply tell them what's right or what's wrong? Why don't you have a position on all of these issues?" But the world is too complex for that. We're not in the business of indoctrination. We're in the business of education. Education implies that the person has within himself or herself the capability of being trained to discern truth. Students aren't simply tapes on which teachers or professors record messages reinforcing their own biases or prejudices. As educators, we trust that what we teach can withstand discussion at every level. And as Christian educators we believe that *God* and *truth* are synonymous. Error cannot stand the scrutiny of prolonged, honest investigation and inquiry. Therefore, we are not afraid to expose Christian truth to any and all scrutiny, knowing, by faith, that in the last analysis Jesus, who is the Truth, shall reign.

More parents need to develop this kind of confidence as they deal with their children. Young people need honest answers to their honest questions. Turning off the mind is not a necessity for the Christian, and *virtue* and *innocence* are not synonymous. Scripture teaches us that we must love God with our hearts *and* our minds (Mark 12:30).

If a parent makes reason take a back seat to rules, the child soon senses that there's no place for using the mind to make discriminating choices. And when that happens, part of God's beautiful creation has been violated.

Truth and Consequences

Sometimes answering the "why?" question involves sitting down and reasoning through the consequences of certain actions, such as taking drugs, or drinking and driving. For a teen, the alternative to satisfactory answers is often unnecessary experimentation. This experimentation in turn leads to guilt and to consequences not easily overcome.

What we see on television is far removed from the cause-and-effect that operates in the real world. For instance, if we tried to drive our cars the way the television private eyes do, we'd soon be dead, or at least our cars would be.

So your son sits down and watches a television program that includes the obligatory chase scene. The *Miami Vice* boys speed up and down the streets at eighty miles an hour. They spin out, fly over ramps, and safely make a two-wheel landing. Night after night he sees variations on this theme.

Well, at some point your boy needs to hear you say, "Don't drive that way, son." But there's more. He also needs to understand why. You need to explain that what Crockett and Tubbs get away with on television has nothing to do with real life. Their high-flying car chases are carefully executed stunts set up by highly trained and skilled professionals using special equipment. Then short segments of film are spliced together to make the scene work. And it won't work with your Ford sedan.

Answering the "why?" question will, of course, take time; and it also calls for a certain amount of self-disclosure, especially when the questions have to do with sexuality.

Getting to the Why

Parent-teen discussions about sexuality need to go much deeper than *how* and *don't*. Young people need to hear a clear *why* behind the *don't*.

Not too many years ago, many parents tried to get away with a simple rule for sexual behavior: "Don't have sex before marriage, or you might get pregnant or make someone pregnant. Or you could contract venereal disease." With the advent of the pill, the condom, and penicillin these threats lost their effectiveness until the AIDS virus surfaced. But these bromides never really addressed the question or the problem.

Society has a difference answer, of course. But the epidemic of venereal diseases, and now AIDS, is tragic proof of the shallowness of the world's answers. Society says, "If it itches, scratch";

"If you want chocolate, eat it"; "If you want sex, do it." Our children deserve better.

Young people need to know something of the why of sexual behavior within a human and Christian context. They need to understand the spiritual implications of giving one's self to another person sexually; they need to have some idea of what it means when two people become one. Teens need to understand that once you indulge or take part in certain intimacies, you can never go back to where you were before. They need to understand that when one of life's deepest experiences becomes simply the satisfaction of an appetite, their own lives are cheapened. The expression of sexual desire outside of marriage, even with moderation, is not condoned by God and for well-stated Biblical reasons.

Teenagers need to understand (as even many adults don't) that God did not hand down the Ten Commandments just to frustrate people. He did not look down and say, "Oooh, look at them; they like that, don't they? I think I'll tell them not to do that! Then they'll climb the walls. But if they do it, I'll smash them." The laws of God are not illogical mandates drawn up whimsically by some uncaring god wielding lightning bolts. They are sensible rules, founded on a Divine logic. In fact, if you sit down and analyze the Ten Commandments, you'll see they are the shortest, most concise, perfect guarantee for the greatest good for the greatest number ever imaginable. They are Divine stop signs.

Traffic signs aren't posted to wreck your transmission. They are placed at intersections as notification of a social contract. And those who ignore them do so at their peril. Just as our kids need to understand why we obey stop signs, they need to understand why we obey God's stop signs, why we don't do what we don't do.

Created As Good and Unique

As we reason through the *why* behind the *don't,* we mustn't lose sight of the inherent goodness of sex as God meant it to be.

Dr. Kenneth Chafin, experienced pastor, teacher, and father writes:

> I've thought a great deal about the attitude which I want my children to have toward sex. At first I developed a long list of concerns, some of which were reflections of my fears for my children. After I thought through each of them, I decided I would settle for two basic attitudes. I would want my children to feel that sex is basically good. Also, I would like for them to think of sex as being very important. I believe that these two attitudes would be good foundations for understanding both the context and nature of the sexual relationship. . . .
>
> A person is never going to experience meaningful sex if he believes that it is dirty or bad. The foundation for all our initial thinking about sex ought to be that it is good. Sex draws its goodness out of the fact that God created it. Looking at all He had created He said, "It is good."[1]

What should we teach our daughters? The value of female anatomy and the importance of their person beyond function and sexuality. What should we teach our sons? That they are not just a littler higher than the animals; they are a "little lower than the angels" and are qualitatively different than other mammals. Teenagers must be taught that our very distinctiveness as human beings is at stake in our sexual conduct. We must think and use our minds not only to operate computers, but to live lives pleasing to God. To think deeply about technology and thoughtlessly about sensuality is dangerous.

My colleague and respected psychologist Dr. Mark P. Cosgrove has real insight into the hand of the Creator in the uniqueness of the human body:

> The most surprising differences between human and animal bodies become obvious when studying sexual activity. The body human tells us very clearly about the importance of our relating as persons in the act of sex. Our culture, on the other hand, has emphasized the animalism of sex at the expense of its personal features. The supposed "naturalness" of the ani-

mal act of sexual intercourse has been used as an argument against those who would support faithful marital sex rather than carnal promiscuity. To deny one's sexual urges has been made to seem unnatural. A close look at nature and the human body, however, suggests a strong personal dimension to human sexual relations. The human sexual response is designed by God for the pleasure and communion of persons.

The body human is designed to allow us to make love face to face, person to person, with prolonged whole-body contact. Human bodies are freed from the enslaving cycles of heat and ovulation to follow the commands of personhood, love, fun, and spirit. The human female is a joint partner in the sex act by the very nature of her body's unique design. She is not just nature's womb in which to plant the seed, but she is an equal partner in the motives, the pleasures, and the communication that is sexual.

Perhaps the mystery of the union of a man and a woman is greater than any of us can know in this life. But we can be sure, as we study the body human, that we have been placed outside the backdrop of animal procreation without losing the joy and pleasure of sex. We can enter into the physical act of sex and, by design, can simultaneously exist a dimension apart from the physical. We can see new perspective and meaning in the physical act of procreation. But we can also look with hope into things only hinted at in the abiding personal union of the marriage bed — two people, yet one, centered on the other, yet never losing sight of self.

A human is the only creature who, as a rule, mates face to face.[2]

That last observation says a great deal about the sanctity of the human sexual act.

What About the Media?

Instead of saying simply, "You can't watch an R-rated-movie," explain why. Discuss it with your teenagers. Use your wisdom, gained through maturity and experience, to explain how the irresponsible behavior depicted in these films creates havoc in the world God loves; explain why such movies fail to uphold a responsible view of the value of human individuals.

As Kenneth Chafin notes:

> Sex is being treated as a toy or a plaything. It is being looked upon as a recreational activity, like bowling. The very casual manner in which people who are almost strangers engage in sex has a way of saying, "It's no big deal." I had the whole philosophy articulated to me with great clarity by a high school student who said without any embarrassment, "It's like any other appetite. If I'm hungry I get a quarter-pounder with cheese, and if I want sex I get a girl who's willing."

Sex is too important a part of life to be reduced to destructive fun and games. It has tremendous potential for good but used carelessly it can be unbelievably disastrous. I would like for my children to have the feeling that while sex is good it is also extremely important and should be treated accordingly.[3]

Nothing New Under the Sun

I think it's a mistake to allow young people to grow up feeling that their parents are naive, like ostriches with their heads in the sand, having no understanding of real life.

For example, each new generation thinks it invented graffiti. But I haven't read anything on the side of a viaduct that I haven't seen before. Sexual perversion is as old as humanity. In fact, if you read the Old Testament from beginning to end, you'll be amazed at the number of "modern" problems and perversions that the nation Israel struggled against. The evil of Sodom goes back to Genesis and is as about as pointed and distasteful a story as one will ever find in any play, novel, television program, or movie.

Your teens need to realize that you are not particularly shocked by nudity. Indeed, you have seen the naked form. They need to understand that you aren't being old-fashioned or foolish in your behavioral requirements. Taboos seem silly unless they are put into context. After all, it's not going to be long before your young person wonders why in one setting it is perfectly fine to look at the human body as a thing of beauty and art or as a source of scientific knowledge about anatomy, yet in another setting it becomes provocatively evil and pornographic.

They need to understand that nudity is not what makes pornography evil. Pornography is evil because it preys upon others, because it victimizes individuals, and because it degrades and perverts God's creation. It treats men and women as no-deposit, no-return commodities rather than unique creations of God.

Sin twists and, ultimately, destroys the beautiful world created by God. Young people must be exposed to these deeper, more far-reaching explanations, rather than simple taboos. For example, when my son started to think about dating, I talked with him about the fact that every girl is somebody's daughter and a child of God. I said things like, "She is His creation. She has a mother, just as you have a mother; she has a father who loves her very much, just as you have a father who loves you. She is somebody's sister, and you know what that means, for you have sisters. Therefore, you must treat her with respect. Just think about the way you would want a boy to treat one of your sisters."

Our teenagers need to know that the standards we set for them are based on the Word of God, not on some old-fashioned, arbitrary guidelines we have established. They need to know what kind of damage irresponsible behavior can do.

Turning to God

Young people need to know, not only the *what* but the *why* and the *who*. They need to know that we do what we do because we are committed to God and because we want to please Him.

Frankly, without Christ our teens are helpless. Turning over the troublesome areas of their lives is an important part of a teen's Christian commitment. For years, Youth for Christ/

Campus Life Ministry leaders have been carefully, painstakingly taking young people through exercises where they commit their minds, their bodies, their relationships, and their emotional lives to God. They say, "God, this is my body. I give it to You. I will not use it in any way that is displeasing to You because I want it to be pure and clean, because You desire that I arrive at marriage with purity."

They also deal with the subject of forgiveness. When young people fail, these leaders help them understand God's grace.

Remember the Old Testament story of Eli? When it came to raising children, this man had a head-in-the-sand attitude; despite his priestly knowledge, he never really confronted his wayward sons with God's truth. Until their tragic deaths, Eli's children lived in rebellion, separated from their father's God.

There's a better way to parent, forthrightly presenting truth and the consequences of wrong behavior and the reasoned *why* behind our rules and boundaries. Please don't think I'm saying there shouldn't be boundaries. Love never participates in the folly of the person being loved. It loves the person, but it never loves the folly. Good parents do not allow their children to persist in foolishness without reminding them that they are playing the fool. Now, the kids may not like being told, and they may pout a little. But you say it anyway, even if they sentence you to two weeks of silence. And eventually they'll come back and say, "Hey, Dad, thanks a lot."

When my son was about seventeen, we took in a troubled youngster for a while. He was an uncontrolled little guy who happened to be the son of one of Chicago's better-known gangsters. In fact, this kid was well on his way to earning the same reputation. Not long after he came to stay with us, my son said to me, "Dad, you know what that kid needs? He needs to live in this house for about six months."

"Why do you say that?" I asked.

"Well, a dose of you would straighten him out."

"What do you mean?" I said. "I thought that you thought I was pretty tough."

"Well, yeah, you're tough, Dad, but we know where we're at all the time. That kid doesn't know where he's at."

Indulgence is not love. Sometimes love says, "I can't go along with this. It's wrong. I love you. You are my child, even if you do this. You can't stop being my child by doing it. But you're doing wrong. You are welcome here in this house. I love you. But I do not countenance what you're doing and here's why."

For about ten years I've carried a copy of a magazine article in my briefcase. Written by an anonymous author, "Misgivings of a Christian Childhood" includes ten things the author wishes his or her parents would have done differently. These words can be a helpful reminder to you, so that these same ten wishes do not become the cry of your sons and daughters when they reach adulthood.

[1] I wish that my parents had known that being a Christian does not necessitate turning off the mind, that innocence is not synonymous with virtue.

[2] I wish that my parents and teachers had known that the Scriptures give broad principles for Christian behavior, not exact and extensive rules for conduct.

[3] I wish that my parents and the church where I grew up had known that sectarian interpretations of various parts of Scripture are not integral parts of the gospel and need not be accepted in totality in order to be a Christian.

[4] I wish my parents had known that there is a difference between being "in the world" and "of the world," and that contact with the world does not constitute worldliness.

[5] I wish that I had learned to take delight in the wonders of the natural world when I was a child!

[6] I wish my parents had known that problems must be solved, not "spiritualized," and that the gospel is not demeaned when we effect solutions by human as well as by spiritual means.

[7] I wish that my parents had known that honest questions, even honest doubts, deserve honest discussion and honest answers.

[8] I wish my parents had known that Christian faith does not guarantee automatic relationships between family members.

[9] I wish my parents had known that while it is possible to hide our prejudices, favoritism, intolerance, and inconsistencies from ourselves, it is not possible to conceal them from children.

[10] I wish my parents had known that unless marriage partners truly love one another, there is little they can teach their children about the love of God or Christian living.[4]

FAILURE TO LET YOUR TEENAGER DEVELOP A PERSONAL IDENTITY

"You Want to Be What?"

I wrote a little essay once called "My Son the Thing," using a bit of overstatement to make a point. "Parents," I said, "don't consider your kid some *thing* that's going to fulfill some aspiration of yours. You couldn't play varsity basketball, but you've bred him for varsity basketball. You remember the day they passed out the letter sweaters and you didn't get one, but you want him to get one. Actually, he wants to play the violin, but you think that's 'twinky.' And you don't want him to be twinky. Not your son. . . . Or maybe you always wanted him to go to college, and he wants to be a plumber. . . ."

The Old Testament story of Saul and David and Jonathan is an interesting study in such misplaced expectations. Saul was a warrior-king. He had maintained control of his kingdom through constant warfare. Then David, a young man from the hills, came to Saul's attention by killing Goliath, a menacing giant. Though David was a shepherd and a musician, he also knew how to fight, and Saul took a real interest in this capable young man. Saul's own son, Jonathan, on the other hand, did not excel in battle. There is no record of him ever receiving any outstanding war honors.

Eventually, David's success on the battlefield made Saul angry not simply because David was threatening his hold on the throne, but because Saul's own son didn't seem to be measuring up in the same way; he didn't seem to be kingly material. To complicate matters, Jonathan and David were close friends, and Jonathan didn't seem interested in quashing David.

At this point, I see Saul as struggling like many fathers today: He could not forgive Jonathan for not being David, and he hated David for not being the son of his dreams. If Saul had not fathered a son himself, the history of Israel might have been a great deal different. Saul might well have adopted David as a son and overseen an orderly succession. Instead, Saul spent years trying to kill his son's best friend.

For me, this story underlines a tremendous error made by many parents. They will not accept their children as individuals, will not accept them for who they are; and beyond this, these parents signal in various ways to the children themselves that they wish they were someone else.

Train Up a Child

"Train up a child in the way he should go: and when he is old, he will not depart from it," says Proverbs 22:6. Until recently, this familiar verse has been interpreted to mean that parents are to make sure that their young people are correctly trained in accordance with the will of God. That is good advice and something for parents to keep in mind.

But Charles Swindoll and others have suggested that in the original Hebrew the intent of this passage is: "Train up a child according to his or her bent." The root word has to do with the bent of a tree. For instance, a willow tree that leans out over a pond toward the southern sun is bent in a certain way. If you try to force it to bend in another way, you will break it.

I see as much wisdom in this interpretation as in the traditional one. Parents should try to raise their children according to Biblical patterns, correcting them and disciplining them so that they understand responsible and obedient behavior. On the other hand, children should be nurtured according to their own bent.

We need to be willing to acknowledge that our children are born with different temperaments and different personality types. I, for instance, cannot conceive of my son standing up to me and defying me in a face-on confrontation. But I can see my younger daughter doing that. Because they're different. If you have three kids in your home, you have three individuals, unique in personality, interests, and talents. Some will succeed in X, while others will succeed in Y.

Within the last generation, researchers have developed tests to determine whether or not a person has abilities in music, art, math, engineering, and many other areas. Through testing, young people can get a good sense of what fields they are best suited for. Solomon didn't have any of these tests available when he wrote his proverbs, of course, but God gave him the wisdom to write the truth.

Devastating Rejection

If a son is athletic and his father was a high school athlete, the two of them will probably have a natural affinity. They'll play catch together, attend games, share the sports page, and generally develop a good father-son relationship. Even if the boy is not a home-run king, the father will be proud of him; he'll sit in the stands and cheer him on and complain, at least to himself, that the coach is just not very wise in not making his son a starter.

But if the father is hanging on to his tattered high-school letter sweater and trying to live out his own dreams through a son who decides to play the flute or, even worse, gets involved in a rock band, the father may signal his displeasure. This kind of rejection is often the beginning of a huge gulf between parent and child. Of course athletic fathers are not the only guilty parties. Musicians, mathematicians, ministers — any parent can project his or her own dreams on to a child with dissimilar bents. Trying to mold the child into the pattern of the parent can be one of the most devastating of all rejections, for the child ultimately feels that nothing he or she does, especially in the areas in which he or she excels, can ever please the parent.

I applaud parents who are willing to discover the bent of their children rather than seeing them as hunks of unsculptured granite to be chipped and chiseled away into the forms they wanted for their own lives.

Showing an Interest

If we've matured beyond our own adolescence, it's our children's happiness that we're seeking, not our own.

Deep within every child is a desire to please the parent. But there is also a competing desire: to be his or her own person and to excel in his or her own areas. The wise parent early learns the inclination of the child and begins to encourage him or her along that line. If the young person shows interest in science and the natural world collecting rocks, insects, butterflies, or hiking in the woods, the wise parent encourages this interest. He or she is willing to look at a parade of bugs and rocks and leaves and moths, thereby giving dignity to the child's natural interest and inclinations.

What really matters is that the parent be a cheerleader who shows enthusiastic interest in the teen's activity. The bridge a parent can build in this way is founded on something more firm than the subject at hand, be it music or sports or rock collecting. The bridge is founded on a parent's obvious pride in and approval of the young person's accomplishments. And this bridge of personal affinity and relationship can carry a parent and child across changed interests later in life.

Many a young person has collected a marvelous array of postage stamps, neatly organized in albums, that eventually end up collecting dust in the attic. However, during a certain period that stamp-collecting hobby was an all-consuming interest, a focal point that, though temporary, was a vital part in the building of the life-long relationship between parent and child.

In some cases, a parent will have to cultivate an entirely new interest. If your kid is crazy about electronics, for instance, you might have to stretch yourself to gather and read some electronics magazines when up to this point you didn't even know how to wire a lamp. But few things draw a parent and child closer than working on a project together in which you are both learning something new. Better yet, let your teenager teach you something; you'll be amazed and vastly rewarded by the joy and accomplishment you sense in your son or daughter.

Remember, the more affirmation and self-esteem a teen gets at home, the less they will need to seek it elsewhere, as the following letter from a teenager attests:

> As most people grow up they are rarely built up and significantly put down causing intense feelings of insecurity and low self-esteem. Whenever someone is encouraged and complimented, he develops a liking for whomever has done this. People have learned how to play on each other's emotions and they will say anything the other wants to hear in order to get the things they want. In my high school youth group I had a good friend named Keri. She had little feeling of self-worth and when Dennis came into her life he made her feel worthwhile. She knew he was an immoral person, had a child already, and had just gotten out of jail, yet she stayed with him because he made her feel good. Keri quit attending church and when I talked to her a few months later she told me she and Dennis were very physically involved. She said, "I know it is wrong but nobody else ever shows love for me in any way and so I am doing whatever it takes to keep Dennis from leaving me." It ripped my heart to see that the world is so cold that many people have to turn to things they don't believe in to feel any personal value.[1]

Nourishing Healthy Dreams

I always feel I've crossed a certain barrier with a young person when, as we've been walking together in the woods or sitting on a log or rocking on the porch of some cabin, suddenly her eyes light up and she begins to share a piece of some dream with me — something she feels might be a little too far-fetched or unreachable, perhaps even a little foolish. I feel honored that the young person has trusted me with his or her wildest hope for the future, and it always makes me think of the lyrics of "To Dream the Impossible Dream."

I've noticed some very unlikely people grow misty-eyed when they hear that song. And I often wonder what those men and women are thinking about. What painful memories does that song evoke? Did someone once squelch their aspirations? Did someone laugh at their dreams? Did they once share something precious, some longed-for goal, only to have a parent say, "No, you can't do it. I want you to be something else"? And did that "road not taken . . . make all the difference"?

I was so saddened one day to hear a very successful doctor, a man I admired because of his medical accomplishments and expertise, admit with tears and with some anger, "I hate what I'm doing. I've always felt God called me to be a missionary. But my dad was unwilling to let me do it because he had spent so much on my education. He said, 'No, you're going to have to make my expenditure worthwhile. The mission field is out of the question.'" This man, at the height of what seemed like a successful career, was regretting the loss of his great dream — a dream his father had overruled.

One of the toughest problems kids from Christian homes face is parents who feel that their kids are going to starve to death if they go into Christian vocations. Or Christian parents who have reached the middle and upper-middle-class income bracket and think that missionaries and pastors should be recruited from the "lower" classes. "If my kid goes into that, she's going to embarrass me because she's going to have to go out and beg for money," they think.

"Merely" a missionary isn't prestigious enough for these parents. Mother imagines a scene where she's having lunch with a member of her country club. Mother asks, "What is your daughter going to do?" And her friend says, "Oh, she's thinking of becoming a brain surgeon." Then the friend asks,

"And what is your son going to be studying?" And Mother is almost embarrassed to have to admit that her son is thinking of going into the ministry. Why? Because being a minister somehow doesn't sound nearly as successful or ambitious or respectable as being a brain surgeon or a lawyer.

Wise parents, however, will turn their children over to God, invite His Holy Spirit to speak to them, and then help them to achieve the goals He implants in them.

Made in God's Image

A lot of people think there's some kind of magic one-two-three formula that will make kids turn out the way you want. That's a destructive cookie-cutter approach to parenting. And often, if you examine the cookie cutter closely, you'll see its the same shape as the person who's wielding it. Unfortunately, there is a lot of arrogance at the root of this attitude: *Wouldn't the world be better if others were made in my shape?*

Fortunately, we are made in the image of God, who is so large, so multi-faceted, so diverse, and so creative that there is room for each of us to develop a personal individuality that will never really encroach on others' territory.

In 1 Corinthians 12 Paul says that God has given each of us different gifts. And as I see it, our God is big enough to have enough gifts to go around. God didn't have to repeat Himself in creation (consider the great variety and diversity in the plants and animals) and He doesn't have to repeat Himself in giving out gifts. Paul goes on to describe the members of Christ's Body as being fitly joined together: hands, arms, torso, neck, eyes, ears. . . . One part, say a hand, cannot say to another, a foot, "I don't need you." God gives His people special and differing gifts and abilities, and all are necessary.

God does not give bad gifts and good gifts; He simply gives different gifts. And when we can accept this in our children, we'll have come a long way toward understanding their uniqueness and toward achieving family harmony.

SIX

FAILURE TO MAJOR ON THE MAJORS AND MINOR ON THE MINORS

"This Room's a Pigsty"

In an attempt to get a laugh, I often use this line with audiences: "In the entire history of America, no child has ever died of 'dirty room.'" Yet not everyone thinks it's funny. In fact, some parents look betrayed—as if I've demeaned them, or stumbled into some forbidden territory, and I have, for many parents make this a major focal point of argument with their children. To ease any tension, I usually follow with, "The national duty of parents is to nag. If a mother doesn't nag about a dirty room or socks on the floor, then she really hasn't been a mother. Mother's need it; kids need it. It's part of the process."

Now I am a believer in boys picking up sock, not mothers picking up socks. And I know that it's much easier to pick up a sock than to teach a boy to pick up a sock. But God didn't create parents to be janitors for teens. When parents become obsessed with neatness or conformity of one kind or another, they are missing the boat. They are majoring on minors.

Think back to the early seventies when boys were wearing long hair. A lot of dads associated long hair with girls, sissies, homosexuals, or political anarchists and communists. A son's long hair was a real threat to the father's sense of control. At the time, preachers and other authority figures were pointing out the negative symbolism of long hair and challenging parents to beware, which only aggravated the parental paranoia.

Many young people didn't — and still don't — know commu-
nism from rheumatism. They were growing long hair because
some rock star was doing it. But parents took this issue on in
full force. I remember one young man saying to me, "We
haven't had a conversation at our dining room table on anything other than hair for months." Now that approach is like
burning down the barn to kill the mice. Or as a former generation put it, "it's winning the battle but losing the war."

Winning the War

Do you remember the story of Joe, back in Chapter 1, who
grew hair because that was the only thing he was good at? Well,
that wasn't the end of the story. We got Joe a job as a janitor in
an office building. I thought a job would be good for him;
maybe he'd learn he could do something else well. It wasn't
long before I got a call from the manager of the office building.

"Say, Joe's been arriving at work a half hour early every
day," he said. "He's supposed to come after the secretaries leave
and then pick up the wastebaskets and do the janitorial work.
But he always comes early."

"Well," I said, "is there anything wrong with arriving a half-
hour early?"

"No. But I just wanted you to know that he doesn't have to
come till later."

When I asked Joe why he was going early every day, he said,
"Well, I've got this plan. They've got all these women working
in that office, and a lot of them are about my mother's age. So I
try to get there before they go home, and when I empty the
wastebaskets, I try to be real nice to them. I overhear them say
things like 'Hey, that kid's pretty nice. Even though he has that
beard and that hair, he's a nice boy.' I just figure that I'll keep
coming early every day until all of them feel I'm a nice guy, and
maybe that will help their kids out a little bit."

Now I tell that story with pride because it obviously says
something special about the character of that young man. But

it always points up a real problem in many homes: there are families that spend all their time on minor matters like hair and how long's long, and how short's short, and how shiny's shiny.

Somehow they don't realize that it's possible for a child to be a conformist on the outside while harboring a deeply disturbed nonconformist on the inside. You know, there's a reason for a release valve on a steam engine. If you let off a little steam, the boiler doesn't blow up. Well, let me tell you, some teenagers can build up a head of steam quicker than any engine. And sometimes these harmless fads provide exactly the release they need.

When I say, "Don't sweat the small stuff," or "Major on the majors not on the minors," you may ask, "Well, what *are* some of the minors and majors?" The "minors" are things like clothing, music, hairstyles, food preferences, and messy rooms. With a little bit of obligatory nagging by parents, most young people will "shape up" in these areas — eventually. "Negative" tastes are probably not going to stay with them the rest of their lives or affect them permanently.

When you're in the throes of it, you, as a conscientious parent, feel as if you're being nibbled to death by minnows, which is an awful way to die. You'd almost rather have be consumed in one big, lion-sized gulp, than to be nibbled to death by all these issues coming at you all at one time. You feel exhausted and battered by the whole thing.

When I was at Youth for Christ, working at summer camps, some adult always asked, "What do you do when the boys raid the girls' cabin?" Or, "What do you do when the boys break a window?"

"I just sleep real well," I'd say. "I don't think a lot about it." When you're fifteen, sixteen, or seventeen, you tend to do dumb things. If you've got a bunch of forty-year-olds doing stuff like this, you've got a problem on your hands. But with sixteen-year-olds — they're just being adolescents.

Teenagers will act like teenagers. They've got short attention spans. They don't keep their promises. They forget — oh, boy, do they ever forget. ("Oh, Mom, I forgot to call!" "Forgot to call?! How could you forget? I've been worried about you all evening!" But your daughter wasn't thinking about you waiting at home for the phone call that would assure you she was all right; she was thinking about whether some boy liked her new dress, or some other big teenage problem.) You cannot expect adolescents to act like adults; you can expect them to act like adolescents. In fact, if they don't, maybe you've got more to worry about than if they do.

Did you ever stop to think that most of the expectations we have of our teenagers are things we've spent our whole lives learning? And that's kind of an insult to us. If they're able to learn in three years something we've spent twenty years learning, they're quite superior — and most of them aren't. Sometimes, we even try to teach them lessons we've never quite learned for ourselves.

One time when I was struggling with some of these very issues myself, I saw a kid on the street dressed up like Paul Revere. I went up to him and asked, "Why are you wearing that costume?"

"This isn't a costume," he said, sounding somewhat affronted. "These are my clothes."

"Don't kid me," I said, "That's a costume. That's not your clothes"

Then he grabbed my tie and said, "Why do you wear that?"

I said, "Well, uh, I wear ties."

"What's their function? Why do you wear them? Are you a conformist? Don't you have any character, any integrity? Can't you be yourself? How come?"

That kid sure gave me something to think about — something I still think about. I wear ties because ties are part of the acceptable attire for executives. I also wear executive-length socks, which bother my kids a lot. They keep asking me, "Are those comfortable, Dad?" Well, I don't wear them for comfort. I wear executive-length socks because the men I know and work with wear executive-length socks. I want to fit in.

Now how is that different from high school? If all the kids are looking like an unmade bed, your kids will want to look like an unmade bed. If all the kids are wearing Levis, your kids will want to wear Levis. And harping at them all the time isn't going to change that. ("What are people going to think if you go to school looking like that? I work my fingers to the bone so you can look like that?" Of course, they bought this stuff at some boutique. It cost thirty bucks to have somebody wear it before they did.)

As I said before, no kid ever died of dirty room. And picking at them all the time probably doesn't help you win the long-term battle.

God Looks on the Heart

Not long ago, Janie and I had plans to go to a church in a nearby town for a Sunday evening service. Mid-afternoon on Sunday we received a call from a college student, who asked, "Would it be all right if a couple of friends and I rode with you to church tonight? We'd like to visit there." As the conversation progressed, I learned that he was the pastor's son. At the appointed time, we stopped at the residence hall to pick up our riders. The young men were ready, but they were all dressed in what I'd call mild punk. With their less-than-conventional haircuts and clothing styles, they did not look like the kind of young people you'd think would want a ride to a Sunday evening church service. But as we talked with them on the way to our destination, Janie and I were both impressed with the quality of their conversation and the kinds of comments they made. In fact, these fine young men were delightful company.

When we got to the church, I wondered if the pastor would appreciate me bringing along his son to the service. I thought, maybe this mode of style and dress is something new—acquired in college—that the father hasn't seen. Maybe he'll be shocked and disapprove. But the parents made no mention whatsoever of the boy's dress or hair. They welcomed him home and were eager to pack up some cookies and other goodies for him to take back to school.

During the evening, I took the mother aside and mentioned how much we had enjoyed meeting the boys and bringing them to church. She commented, "You know, our son has never been the slightest problem to us. We're so proud of him. He's a good student. He's caring toward us and his grandparents. He's a loving older brother to our other children. And he's a sincere, devoted Christian."

Considering the fact that I get a great deal of mail from parents encouraging me to apply a stronger dress code at the university, this experience provided a great lesson for me. I'm bombarded with, "If you were really following Christ, you would force those kids to cut their hair differently and to wear different clothing," and so on. But, thanks to those young men, I now have a stock answer: As long as our young people are devoted to their parents and to God, as long as they are respectful to others and conscientious about their school work, I don't think it matters very much how they dress.

One of the things I discovered in talking with those young men was that they were trying to make a statement with their unconventional dress style. They were trying to say, "You can't tell a book by its cover." And indeed, it's wise to find out what a person's real values are before you attack his or her appearance. On the other hand, you can never assume that someone who dresses in a conventional manner and looks scrubbed clean has an equally right and clean heart before God. Jesus surely made the opposite point. In Matthew 23:27, He called the Pharisees whitewashed tombs that looked beautiful but were full of death.

I repeatedly encourage parents not to make the mistake of majoring on minors and allowing the more important issues to slip by.

The Majors

What are the important issues on which a parent should focus? Many of them are topics I've discussed in other chapters of this book: respect for authority, including God, the government, and parents; developing a giving, generous spirit; honesty; integrity; trustworthiness; stick-to-itiveness. Along with these, however, goes an overarching issue, and that is the matter of building a child's self-image. Self-image is important not simply because it makes for happier, more self-fulfilled teenagers. It goes much deeper than that. The way your children perceive themselves will have a great effect on how they perceive and relate to other people.

Listen to what Donald Sloat has to say about the importance of a positive self-image:

> Some people take exception to the idea that Christians should have good self-esteem because they equate positive self-esteem with sin. . . . I believe many people are confusing self-esteem or self-image, a part of our psychological equipment, with our inability to earn salvation, a spiritual concept. I can have good self-esteem and still recognize that my righteousness is "like filthy rags" (Isaiah 64:6). Conversely, calling myself a worm is not going to earn any spiritual points, either. Often I see Christians beating themselves on their heads, putting themselves down, and treating themselves horribly in the name of God. As author David Seamands says with great wisdom:
>
> "The truth is that self-belittling is not true Christian humility and runs counter to some very basic teachings of the Christian faith. The great commandment is that you love God with all your being. The second commandment is an extension of the first — that you love your neighbor as you love yourself. We do not have two commandments here, but three: to love God, to love yourself, and to love others. I put *self* second, because Jesus plainly made a proper self-love the basis of a proper love for neighbor. The term *self-love* has a wrong connotation for some people. Whether you call it self-esteem or self-worth, it is plainly the foundation of Christian love for others. And this is the opposite of what many Christians believe."[1]

People who don't firmly grasp the fact that they are made in God's image have a hard time acknowledging — in word or in action — that other people are made in God's image.

In her book *You Can Be Your Own Child's Counselor,* Elizabeth Skoglund elaborates on what the Bible has to say about self-esteem, especially as it relates to teens.

There is biblical evidence for the rightness of a proper self-image. Paul on several occasions shows pleasure over his accomplishments. In Romans 15:17, 18 he says, "So it is right for me to be a little proud of all Christ Jesus has done through me. I dare not judge how effectively He has used others, but I know this: He has used me to win the Gentiles to God." Again in Romans 12:6 Paul says, "God has given each of us the ability to do certain things well." The obvious implication is that we are to be aware of our strengths and appreciate them.

But self-esteem is more than just liking certain isolated characteristics about ourselves. Thus, at the end of his life, Paul could say to Timothy, "I have fought long and hard for my Lord, and through it all I have kept true to Him" (2 Timothy 4:7). He expresses a contentment that is appropriate and right.

Just the fact that God is a God of truth is evidence enough of God's approval of us when we have a good honest estimate of ourselves. It is not a virtue to say that I am not good at my job, if I am good at it. Nor is it right to deny any other good point about myself. Self-esteem, to be real, must be based on an honest evaluation of oneself. To be dishonest is certainly not Christian.

A teenage girl who is a brilliant pianist told me that, while she knows she's good at playing the piano, she feels wrong about her awareness of that ability. Sometimes she goes so far as to try to play poorly so that she won't be so proud! Understandably, this drives her teacher to distraction and is not in the end a very good example of Christianity.

Low self-esteem doesn't make anyone appealing to others and it becomes the height of self-occupation, which is the very thing the Bible speaks against. People who dislike themselves are not humble, they are self-occupied. They are continually concentrating on their failure, their supposed lack of worth. In contrast, people who like themselves are self-forgetful.

One seventh-grade girl who, because of her low self-image, hates social situations, goes home after a party and rehearses the whole evening in her mind. She, of course, always comes out looking badly to herself.

Thus a person with low self-esteem frequently spends painful hours concentrating on real or, more often, imagined slights and criticisms from those around him. Indeed, he is so occupied with himself that he can hardly pay any attention at all to others. Yet paying attention to those around us is a primary scriptural command.[2]

In working with young people you see many kids who are very handsome, athletic, or beautiful and who have everything that most of us want going for them. And yet some of those same kids are unbelievably lacking in self-esteem; many even have real contempt for themselves. On the other hand, you meet some rather plain kids with relatively modest talents who have very healthy self-images.

This remains one of the great mysteries for people who work with youth. What makes an "average" young person so self-assured, confident, and winsome, and another who has so many natural gifts so self-denigrating, even self-loathing? I believe if you were to dig into the family backgrounds, you would find that those who have healthy self-esteem live in homes filled with trust, respect, and affirmation.

In *The Rejection Syndrome,* Charles Solomon emphasizes the important influence a parent can have in molding a child's self-image.

Alienation from oneself or rejection of oneself is a common phenomenon. Typically, most of our attitudes about ourselves are more learned than innate. We tend to value ourselves as others value us and we see ourselves as others see us or, at least, as we perceive their evaluation and assessment of us.

Those who have been rejected by others are set up emotionally to reciprocate by displacing the rejection they feel onto those around them who may have no idea why they are being rejected. Those rejected from early childhood usually learn their lessons well and reject themselves in varying facets of their lives.

Such alienation or self-rejection may take the form of interpreting feelings of inferiority as fact rather than feeling. Putting oneself down, being critical of one's accomplishments, and self-hatred are some of the indicators of self-rejection.

Those suffering alienation from themselves or self-rejection will foster such attitudes in their children. It is easy to see why the sins of the fathers can be passed on to the children and to the third and fourth generations.

Apart from a full understanding and appropriation of the grace of God in redemption, the alienation which is common to man will drive him to seek substitute answers. In many cultures it takes the form of attempting to appease evil spirits or some false deity. Each culture has some religious exercise through which its members attempt to bridge the gulf of alienation.

Alienation from God, others, and ourselves can only be bridged through the finished work of Calvary—redemption, reconciliation, and acceptance found in Christ.[3]

Developing Self-Esteem

How do we develop a positive self-image in young people? Let me suggest three ways in addition to the ones I mention elsewhere in the book (particularly in Chapter 7).

1. Respect their opinions. You could parachute me onto a desert island filled with teenagers and I could tell you which ones have been respected at home around the table, which ones have been listened to, which ones have parents who allow them to speak, which ones have parents who do not always have to be right. Kids who have lived in homes where their opinions have been respected, and where they've been allowed to speak, have a certain manner about them. They can communicate with adults. In contrast, the others tend to withdraw and simply do not know how to deal with adults. Wise parents discuss ideas with young people and help them develop an opinion based on careful thought and fairness. Young people whose opinions are respected tend to develop a positive self-image.

No one enjoys talking with somebody who always makes it obvious that he or she is superior. And in king-of-the-hill conversations, the kid *always* loses.

With teenagers, I try to ask questions that draw them out: How do you feel about this? What's your opinion on this subject? What are the kids at school saying about this? They can answer those questions without feeling they're being judged for a right or wrong response. Everybody can *feel* a certain way. Everybody has an opinion.

With our family altar, we had a system that worked pretty well. We'd sit around the table, and after presenting a subject, I'd start with the youngest child and ask, "What do you think about that?" After the youngest had said something, I'd turn to the middle child and say, "What do *you* think about it?" Well, he, being a little older, could usually come up with something a little better than his sister. Then I went on to the oldest and said, "What do you feel about that?"

Now if you start with the oldest and she unloads the whole thing, the smaller kids feel the pressure of not having enough to contribute. But this way, every child has a chance to give an opinion on his or her own level.

2. Respect their property. There's an age-old discussion about property rights versus personal rights. But I think they are the same thing. Personal rights can't exist in a vacuum. Everyone I've ever met who has had a home broken into has felt that his or her own personhood has been violated. Even if they weren't at home when it happened, they felt personally assaulted. Why? Because our property is an extension of our person.

People must have a certain respect for things in order to have respect for themselves or for others. Have you had kids walk into your home and immediately show disrespect for your furniture, put their feet on the end tables, put their legs over the arm of the chair? Those kids probably didn't own anything that was really theirs. They'd never been taught to respect anything and have that sense of "I've got to take care of this because it's mine."

Kids who are given a pet or a bicycle or clothing that's their very own, that they can care for and be proud of, tend to develop a self-esteem on the basis of this respect of property. Then that property should be respected by others in the family.

Say your kid has a bike. You gave it to her as a gift for Christmas, and, come July, you want to ride it. You ought to say, "May I borrow your bike?" instead of assuming that what's hers is yours. That respect of property is really a respect of personhood.

Kids who are allowed to grab each other's things and use them without permission generally don't understand their own person. Daughters need to be taught to ask before they borrow a sister's sweater. You don't just go rummaging from room to room looking for people's things. And that goes for parents as well as siblings.

As a parent respects a young person's room, collections, wall hangings, and so forth, that young person will sense that the parent doesn't violate his or her person. That teen will learn what it means to respect the property of others.

3. Respect their privacy. We also build up a person's self-image by respecting their privacy. Frequently I get letters that include something like this: "I just happened to be going through my boy's dresser, and I just happened to look at the section underneath the drawer, and I just happened to find these girlie magazines. What should I do?"

Well, first of all I tell them that their son is probably not a budding pervert; he's probably just a curious young male who wants to know what women look like, and he'll probably outgrow that. But I also say that before they raise the issue of the magazines with their son, they'd better acknowledge the fact that they've violated his privacy. I would say, "Son, I have a problem. I have an ugly, nasty, awful case of the normals. I am a caring father (or mother). I have a normal curiosity. I love you so much, I don't want you hurt. I've been fearful about some things and my curiosity got out of hand and I went into your room and I snooped around. Will you forgive me for that?" Usually they will, fast. After that, you deal with what you found.

In an article in *McCall's* Billy Graham said that he had never entered any of his children's bedrooms without asking permission. Now that is a high standard. I could not say that for myself. I have occasionally burst into somebody's room when I shouldn't have.

I understand that the worst thing about solitary confinement in a prison camp is not necessarily the solitary part. The worst part of it is that the guards might open the door at any moment, no matter what you're doing — tending to your personal hygiene, anything — and watch you. You start feeling like a cockroach moving around the walls. It tears down your personhood. You feel subhuman because you have no privacy. All human beings need privacy, including our children.

Trust them with some leisure time. Allow them to spend time in their rooms thinking. If someone's badgering and picking all the time — "What are you thinking? What are you doing?" — they have no opportunity to develop a wholesome and personal interior life.

Some of what goes on in the sanctity of a soul is far too private to be shared with anyone else. Most of us, at one time or another, try to write poetry or music. Most of us aren't any good at it, but that attempt is a cry of the soul to make a valued, creative contribution. Young people who have time to struggle with and work through these issues tend to develop a better sense of self-worth than those who are robbed of their times of solitude and personal privacy.

Laying a Foundation

I talk a lot about respect, and for a good reason: children grow up to treat others as they've been treated. More is caught than taught.

If you concentrate on the majors instead of the minors, you'll lay a solid foundation that will support your sons and daughters throughout their lives.

In *Adolescence Is Not an Illness*, Bruce Narramore gives eight good guidelines for determining how to set limits — on the major issues.

1. Recognize that every person is different. What was right for you when you were a teen, or what is right for one teen is not necessarily suitable for another.

2. Discuss the possible limits with your teenager before making a decision. If your mind is already made up and you don't really listen to your son or daughter's perspective, he or she will know you are simply defending your position, rather than really looking at the situation with an open mind.

3. Differentiate between a biblical absolute and your personal preference. Sometimes we parents just naturally assume that our way of looking at things is the biblical way. Whether it is hair length, clothing styles, or forms of entertainment, we conclude that we have the final word on the issue. Many teenagers have been turned off by parents who thought they were being helpful by claiming that certain forms of dress or certain social activities were obviously sinful and out of God's will. If we are convinced that a certain style of dress or an activity like movies or dancing is not helpful, we should tell our teenagers why we think so. And we can share with them our reasons. But we must take great care not to tell them the Bible clearly supports our position, unless God has in fact clearly spelled it out in Scripture. Our teens can read for themselves and are likely to be very resentful, when they start reading the Bible for themselves and find out we have been putting words in God's mouth!

4. Be flexible. There are reasonable exceptions to most rules. A special situation with proper safeguards may call for revised limits.

5. Compare your standards to those of a variety of other parents. This can help avoid narrow decisions. It can also help see where we may want to set limits that other parents haven't.

6. Work toward cooperative development of standards. Don't get in the position of being a policeman or a judge. You are a loving, caring parent, who wants to work together with your teenager for his good.

7. Allow increased freedom and responsibility with age. Sixteen-year-olds can generally make better decisions than they could at fourteen, and their responsible choices are encouraged by growing freedom to form decisions.

8. Never set a limit without giving a good reason. "Because I said so!" is a frustrating reason to growing, fair-minded teenagers. They are bright enough to understand our reasons even if they don't agree. We will develop their abilities to make decisions by giving a clear answer to their question *Why?*[4]

SIX

FAILURE TO COM-
MUNICATE APPROVAL
AND ACCEPTANCE

"Can't You Do Anything Right?"

A friend of mine tells about the time he went to his local school for the second-grade open house. On display were all these little ceramic creations the kids had made in art class. They had molded them out of clay, mixed various colors, painted them, and then, with the teacher's help, fired them in the kiln. At the open house the children presented their creations to their parents.

As my friend explains, these dishes had permanently glazed fingerprints all over them. The colors were laid on unevenly. And the bottoms usually didn't sit flat. Nonetheless, they were the work of loving fingers, proudly given.

My friend walked out of the school about the same time as another family. The little boy was all smiles, walking with his parent, carrying his dish toward the parking lot. But suddenly the boy tripped on the step and fell. The dish, his cherished piece of second-grade art, shattered into a hundred pieces, and the child began to cry. Of course the parent picked up the child and tried to console him. But the words didn't seem to come out right. "Now don't cry, it's nothing. It was just a dish. It doesn't matter."

As my friend saw the situation—and I agree—this parent obviously loved the child, yet had a deep misunderstanding of the human spirit. Yes, the parent loved the child and wanted to console him, but went about it the wrong way. For that dish did matter. It was not simply an expendable piece of clay. To that child it represented his creativity, his life, his accomplishment. It did matter. A wiser parent might have said, "Oh, that's awful! Isn't it terrible that the dish is broken. Let's pick up all the pieces and see if we can put them together. It was such a beautiful dish, and I'm so sorry that it broke." To ignore the dish was to ignore the child and, in some way, depreciate his long and loving efforts.

In a less dramatic way, virtually everything our young people try to do can be compared to that ceramic dish.

When a boy runs into the outfield to catch a ball and it lands in his glove, he looks toward the grandstand — because he wants to see one smiling face. He wants to see a "thumbs up" from the one supreme person in life, his parent.

Young people need to be affirmed, to be told that what they are doing meets with our standards and is pleasing to us. As they are wondering where to go and where to put their efforts, this helps motivate them to achieve, to accomplish, and to grow.

A Subtle Disinterest

Someone has properly said that the opposite of love is not hate; the opposite of love is indifference. It's safe to say that few, if any, parents have hated their child, but many have been indifferent to their child's interests. When you never get up from the chair and walk across the room to look at something that has been laid out in Legos or blocks, when you never admire a picture that has been colored within the lines, when you never listen with interest to a new song that has been learned, you set a negative tone of rejection.

Later, teenagers often will hide their accomplishments from parents because they feel or fear this subtle rejection. The parent has not been interested before, so why should it be any different this time? Parents say to me, "I can't get my teenagers to talk. They won't tell me about their lives." Sometimes kids shut their parents out because of this kind of early-childhood rejection. As far as they have it figured, anything they say to the parent will be judged unimportant or childish.

I've known of families in which a young person has died and afterward the parents, digging through the room, find surprising traces of the young person's interests. They knew nothing of a notebook filled with poetry, a collection of items scrounged on vacation, a diary that reveals deep longings for parental acceptance. Parents have come to me and said, "I didn't have any idea. I didn't know what he was doing when he was alone."

There's one scenario I've repeatedly experienced with teenagers, and it always grieves me: Young people will show me their yearbooks as if they were desperate for approval. These kids know exactly how many times their pictures appear in the books. Sometimes it's only once—in the pages lined with individual portraits and the accompanying list of high-school list of accomplishments underneath the picture. Too many times I've read over those lists and heard the young person say, "My dad doesn't have any idea how many things I've been involved in in school. He's never come to a ball game or a play or a concert. He doesn't know the hours I've spent in science club or in debate or gymnastics." They say these things with lumps in their throats, and I am painfully aware of how much they wish that their parents only understood how all-important these interests were.

I once had a woman say to me, "My husband has destroyed me." I prepared myself for a story of physical abuse and unusual mental torture, but that wasn't the case at all. "Every time I try to tell him about my concerns around the house—maybe I need a faucet fixed or the screen door is broken or the garage door opens crooked—and try to tell him I need some help, he simply says, 'Call a man. Tell him about it. Don't bother me with that.' He has taken everything that I'm interested in and put it in a category labeled *unimportant*. He doesn't understand that my life is the sum total of all these small, seemingly unimportant activities. He's put them all in a bundle and rejected them, which means he's rejected me. He's destroyed me."

The hurt and anger I saw in her reminded me of my many trips through high-school yearbooks with students desperately seeking approval. Nothing will make a son or daughter feel less important than to have his or her seemingly small interests ignored by parents.

Taking a Personal Interest

In trying to train and equip youth workers over the years, Campus Life has always encouraged them to personalize their ministry. Relational evangelism is far more effective than preaching at young people or condemning them for certain behavior. Those alternatives simply don't work. They may make the evangelist feel better, but they won't win young people to the Savior.

The youth workers spend time getting to know young people. They read the school paper. They find out what the kids have been up to. They arrive early at the meeting, and when a boy walks in who has been on the dean's list or the honor roll, they say, "Hi, John. Hey, I was reading about you in the school paper. I saw that you made the honor roll." Or, "Hey, I noticed you became treasurer of the Latin Club." Or, "Nancy, I see that you're playing in the band contest next month." Or, "Jim, you guys sure played hard Friday night. That was a pretty close game. Tough team. Sorry you lost, but I was real proud of the way you played." The youth worker who takes the time to gather this kind of information about every single young person will be the most effective youth worker.

With some kids, of course, you've really got to scramble to find something to notice and affirm. Maybe, "I noticed that you've got a different car." Or, "How do you like your new job?" It doesn't seem too important what the issue is, just as long as you take notice of their achievement and take the time to make a personal and positive observation of their behavior or accomplishment.

Now that we're in the university setting, Janie and I have been amazed at how much even college young people need this. On a Saturday afternoon we will walk over to a track meet to watch the girls compete; and by Tuesday we will have received five or six cards through the mail thanking us for coming to the meet and giving them our support. Every time we watch a baseball game or a basketball game we receive notes like that through the mail. We're just there as part of the crowd, but somehow the kids do notice and feel affirmed.

Sometimes after the team has lost a football or basketball game I hardly know what to say. It would be so much easier to walk away from the field or out of the gym and go home than to stay and greet the disappointed players. But I've found that just walking through the locker room, putting a hand on a shoulder or shaking hands, communicates meaningfully.

For years as I've gone to youth camps to minister the Gospel, I've always tried to find the most negative kids — the kids who are on the edge of things and not fitting in. I just kind of hang around them a bit or walk up to their group and say, "Hello, how are you doing?" Maybe I notice somebody's funny hat or pick up on something someone says or even let myself be the brunt of a joke. Then the next time I see them, I walk up and say something about the last conversation. In the course of a five-day retreat or camp, I can almost always win these kids over. They will either make a commitment to Christ, or they will come up to say good-bye and tell me they hope to see me again next year. "Hey, do you think you'll be down here again? Could we visit you sometime at your place?" It never ceases to amaze me how little affirmation it takes to win kids over to the place where they desire a relationship.

Many adults say, "You must have some kind of magic to be liked so well by kids." But I see it as quite the opposite. It's not magic at all. You show interest in them, and they will begin to show interest in you.

A Spoonful of Sugar

I once worked with a man known for never complimenting any of his co-workers or staff. One day I said to him, "You know, one of your staff mentioned to me that you've never said 'thank you' for anything he's ever done, and that you rarely hand out compliments."

"That's right," he answered. "Whenever I do give a compliment, they'll know they've earned it. But until they do a very outstanding piece of work, they'll not get praise from me."

At heart his philosophy had a lot going for it. "Cheap" or undeserved compliments, false flattery, aren't worth much. But encouragement and affirmation are something else. Everyone needs a pat on the back now and then; and this is especially true with adolescents. And even criticism can be given in a loving and caring manner, privately, with four or five sentences of affirmation and approval for every one sentence of disapproval or correction.

A friend once commented, "Jay, there are more sugar horses in the world than whip horses." How very true. A pointed illustration of this was given in a farewell speech made by one of the young editorial staff members of *Campus Life* magazine as he was leaving to go to another position.

The young writer said, "I so appreciate Harold Myra." (At the time, Harold was the editor of the magazine.) "Where I used to work, when I made a mistake, the editor would write through it with a heavy black pencil. He would make arrows all over the paper and write things beside the sentences like 'Unclear' or 'Sloppy' or 'You can do better than this' or 'This is terrible, rewrite.' "

This young writer went on to say, "Everyone of those big black pencil marks was like a dagger cutting away at my heart. The thing I've enjoyed about working with Harold Myra is that, though he has a high standard as an editor, he always writes in light pencil and with very small letters beside the sentence, 'Try this' or 'Perhaps you could add something to this' or

'Maybe you'd like to rethink this paragraph.'" He said he appreciated not only the kindness of the phrases but also the lightness of the pencil and the smallness of the letters. "It seemed as if I was being helped and lifted rather than being cut down. I wanted so hard to please him and do a good job."

Harold Myra knew how to bring out the best in that young person.

Practice Saying the Words

To say to your child, "I'm proud of you. That was a good job. I'm so happy that you're my child" provides more positive reinforcement than almost anything you could ever do. Some parents say, "It's hard for me to do this. I always see the negative. I don't see the positive."

And I say to them, "Practice. Try mouthing the words. Blurt it out. Say it. Take a risk. You'll be glad you did." Even when a young person has tried and failed, a parent should take him aside and say, "I know how very much you wanted to do this, and I know how hard you tried. I saw how you put your whole self into it. And even though you didn't win, I was very proud of the way you did it—of your composure, your sportsmanship, and the way you conducted yourself even in the midst of disappointment. I'm very proud of you."

A young man once told me, "I don't care how well I do on the yard—I can do the whole yard, trim all the bushes, trim around all the trees, do the best job possible—when my dad pulls in the driveway, he doesn't see the yard. He just sees that one little clump of grass that I missed. He harps on that and never even mentions all the other work I've done all day long. It really discourages me and makes me feel like just giving up and not doing anything at all. Why put in all that work if you're going to get chewed out anyway?"

What if that father had just once said, "Hey, great job." Or if it wasn't a "great" job, why not notice the boy's tenacity and industry? What if he had just commented on how much time it must have taken the boy to do all that work and thanked him for it, or complimented the boy in the presence of a neighbor or a friend? What would that have meant to the son?

That little phrase — "I'm proud of you" — has unbelievable power. But it must be said, not just thought.

My dad was part of a generation of men who found it difficult to express affection openly. I remember the first church meeting we attended where they asked people to hold hands and sing. Dad thought we were being asked to do something perverted. He had never held hands with a man in his life, and he couldn't do it and sing! He was a real man's man. Now Dad hadn't missed a Notre Dame game since 1921, and after every game I'd call him and we'd go over it play by play. Then a few years ago, about three years before he died, at the end of our phone calls Dad started saying, "Jay, I love you." It had taken him years to be able to express his love for me that blatantly, and even though we had had a wonderful relationship, those three words meant everything to me.

When I think of the importance of those three words, I recall a home where I once visited. There were three boys in the family. The oldest was a student at an Ivy League school and was very sophisticated; all through supper he kept using polysyllabic words. The youngest was a freckly little delight, kind of like Huck Finn. And then there was the middle one.

The middle kid was about twelve and kind of surly. You know, surly to bed, surly to rise — generally, a nasty sort. I was a visiting preacher, and this kid was constantly embarrassing his parents in front of me. They kept trying to shut the little character up, but it didn't work.

When the meal ended and the boys left the room, the father immediately said, "You see our problem?"

"What do you mean?" I asked innocently.

"The middle one."

"Well," I said, "he's got a real handicap. He lives in between these bookends. He's got this big brother who is real impressive with his college talk and this cute little brother everyone loves.

But he's at that age where he's about as exciting as unsalted mashed potatoes when compared to his brothers. So he's trying all these attention-getting devices." I let that sink in a minute and then added, "Do you ever tell this boy that you love him?"

"Well . . . we're not that kind of family," the parents said.

"I don't mean getting mushy in front of all his buddies. But it's real important to learn to tell him you love him." They asked me how they might do this, and I said, "Every day each of you should tell that boy in English — in words that he can under-stand — 'I love you.' There are lots of ways you could do this. For instance, when he gets into bed at night, go into his room, sit on the edge of his bed, and say something like, 'You know, I've been thinking, if we had all the twelve-year-old boys in town lined up in a row, we'd take you again. I want you to know something: I love you.' He won't fight that, believe me. Find a way to tell him you love him every day."

Well, two or three months later I got a letter from those parents. "Jay," they said, "thank you, thank you. It's been such a big help. You can't believe. It's transformed that boy."

Family Affirmation

It works. And healthy homes are homes where family members learn to express their love and affirm each other — husband to wife, parents to children, even *children to children.*

"Oh, boy," you may say. "How do you get siblings to affirm one another?" First of all, let me make it clear that I'm not de-fining *love* as something you feel but as something you do.

Children can learn to build each other up. For instance, in our family no one is allowed to "bag" another — talk about him or her in the third person. Once somebody's in that "bag," you can really do him or her in.

When our kids would get angry at each other — or at one of us — they'd start making accusations around the dinner table: "*He* did this," or "*she* said that." Then Janie would say, "Now who are you talking about?" She'd make them say, "*Laurie* said this." "*Bruce* did that." "*Terri* said this." Or even (and often) "*Daddy* said that."

During adolescence, when siblings are fighting all the time, a responsible attitude toward each other—even something as seemingly simple as putting a name and a face on an accusation—is a big step toward affirming one's personhood.

What's in a Name?

I sometimes play a game with adults and ask them to tell the name that their parents used for them in fun when they were children. The response is always interesting. Those who were given positive or "cute" names, like Cricket or Pigeon or Dolly or Peachy, tend to be smiling, radiant, happy people. Those who were nicknamed Toad or Turkey or Fats are often the opposite.

One could ask, of course: "Were these names used to describe certain characteristics?" Probably so. But did the names then become self-fulfilling prophecies? Probably so.

When I go through this exercise with a group of young adults, there are usually a few quiet ones and some with tears. Some will angrily comment, "I would never do that to my child."

I'm sure Jesus knew the importance of names when He looked at Simon, an impetuous man given to temper tantrums (someone has said that Peter got most of his exercise flying off the handle and jumping to conclusions), and said, "Simon, I'm going to rename you Peter, the rock, and upon this rock I will build My church" (Matthew 16:18). How this must have confused the other apostles. This man whose life was like Jell-O was being called a rock? But I believe that from that moment on Peter determined to live up to that name. And, indeed, he did. Oh, he may have failed at times; like all of us, he had his highs and lows. But by the time he wrote his two epistles—and you can surely sense it in his words—Peter had become the kind of solid believer upon whom the church of Jesus Christ can be built. He had become a man who could carry the keys to the kingdom.

For good or bad, parents can label their teenagers. And with those labels we can express our love and acceptance — or our subtle disapproval and disregard.

Matter of Trust

Children raised in an atmosphere of suspicion and distrust will eventually say, "If that's the kind of son he thinks I am, that's the kind of son I'm going to be." They cannot live past their parents' expectations.

Young people develop trustworthiness by being trusted. Parents who provide children with opportunities to be trusted from the time they are very small, and who continue to add more and more weight to the trust they give their teenagers, will be amply rewarded. Most kids will break their backs to earn their parents' trust. But kids who are continually met with "What's the real story?" eventually give up; they lose heart. Few things are more damaging to young people than this kind of overwhelming mistrust and suspicion.

With our one son, Janie and I discovered that we kept saying no to him all the time. One day he came to me and said, "Dad, you guys say no to everything."

"No, we don't!" I said.

"You do! You say no to—"

"You get to do a lot of things," I said. "You've got a lot of freedom."

But that conversation made Janie and me take a look at our attitude. (Of course we always did this in private and then came out looking as if we agreed, even if we didn't.) What we discovered was a lack of trust on our part. We didn't know what was on our son's mind, so when he asked us something, we suspected there was more to it. If we said yes, we were going to get conned. If we said no, we could buy time. No seemed easier than, "Well, let me think about that a little longer," or, "When do you need a decision on that?" We were saying no so often that we were using up our equity.

My theory is, you say yes to everything you can say yes to, and then when you've got something really important to say no to, you come *down* with no. That way your teens realize that you don't say no very often—but when you do say no you really mean no. But if you are using *no* to buy time, you soon use up your equity and have nothing left in the bank anymore. You've spent it all.

It's very hard to trust under certain circumstances.

I well remember the day one of our daughters got her license—we had the worst snowstorm of the year that day, and she wanted to take the car! "Daddy, can I take the car to the basketball game?"

"Dear Lord," I prayed. But I said yes. By half-time there was six inches of snow on the ground, and I was one worried dad. So I got in the other car, drove to the school, and sat in the parking lot, and I waited for her to come out so I could follow her home.

Boy, was I in for a surprise. First of all, my daughter did things I would never do. In the winter I clear a small hole on the windshield, turn on the wipers, and start out; as long as there's a tiny hole I can see out of, I drive. But my teenage daughter swept every window off, all around the car. She scraped the windows, warmed up the car—did everything by the book before she took off.

I followed her for a little ways. When it finally dawned on me that she knew what she was doing, I suddenly zipped down a side street to try to get home before she did. I just made it!

Believe me, I know how hard it is to trust your kids on certain things. When your daughter comes home from a date, you always check to make sure everything's zipped and buttoned in the right buttonholes.

As soon as my daughters would leave the house on a date, I would start worrying. I was like a water tank with a fire under it; as soon as they were out the driveway, little bubbles would start rising in my tank. By the time they got home at the end of the evening, I was at a full boil. "Where have you been? What have you been doing?" I'd give them what they called the third degree.

To ease everyone's tension, Janie and I tried some advice we read somewhere, and it worked. Before our teens went out, we established what time they should be home. (We also established with the girls' dates that one place our daughters didn't go was "out." "Out" was too big a place. We wanted it narrowed down a little. You don't go "out"; you go to a certain place, and you come home at a certain time. I wasn't as concerned about some magic curfew hour as I was about knowing what time a certain event got out and what time I could expect them home.) Anyway, we put an alarm clock in the bathroom — the first place they went when they got home. So if they were to be home by 11:30, we'd set the alarm for 11:30. If they got home before 11:30, they'd simply turn off the alarm. No problem. But if they came home after 11:30 I'd hear the alarm clock. Then I'd get up — and sit on the tub until they got home. This way my bubbles only had to boil for a little while.

It really worked. I trusted that they were where they'd said they'd be — until they stepped over the line. Then I started to worry.

I had a kid come up to me once and say, "Jay, can you explain my dad?"

"What do you mean, explain your dad?" I asked.

"He does the most unpredictable things."

I said, "Like what?"

"Well, I was driving down the road, and somehow I forgot about this railroad crossing. When I got there, this train went by, and I hit the brakes and my car — my dad's car — turned around on a dry pavement — did a whole circle — and came to a stop rear end toward the train, almost on the tracks. I was weak. I made promises to God, and I came home and gave the keys to Dad. 'Dad,' I said, 'I don't think I'm ready to drive the car.' I told him what had happened, and you know what he did?

He gave the keys back to me. He said, 'Now you're ready to drive. You weren't really ready before, but now you are.' "

We teach our kids to be trustworthy by trusting them with the smaller things. Then we can trust them with the bigger things.

What's a Parent To Do?

In his book *What's A Parent To Do?* Gordon McLean sums up ways to affirm a young person. Most of his list focuses on the little considerations that make a huge difference in a person's self-esteem, and I've paraphrased them for you here. I challenge you to give them a try.

Treat your teenager courteously.

Say *please* and *thank you* instead of just giving orders.

Use the name or nickname your teenager prefers.

Treat your teenager's possessions with respect and don't use them without his or her permission. This will help teach your teen to place a value on the belongings of others.

Presume they are telling the truth until it has been proven otherwise.

Compliment them when they do a task well.

Teach by example that you do not discriminate against another person because of the color of skin or cultural or economic background. Teach your teens to appreciate the customs and traditions of racial and national groups other than their own.

Give them work they can perform successfully, and help them if they need it.

Use constructive criticism to correct a fault or error, not to destroy self-confidence.

Recognize their right to privacy and respect their confidence.

Give serious consideration to their interests and questions.[1]

FAILURE TO APPROVE YOUR TEENAGER'S FRIENDS

"Where Did You Find Him?"

As I've polled young people in camps, conferences, and Campus Life settings over the last three decades, I've repeatedly heard this common complaint against parents: "My parents won't accept my friends."

Adult that I am, I sometimes quote back to them the cliché: "We're known by the company we keep."

And they frequently say, "Yeah, but my folks don't even know what my friends are really like. If they knew them, they'd like them. They write them off on the basis of their dress, the way they talk, or the homes they come from. They don't bother to get to know them. They just tell me they don't want me to run around with that kid because they heard something about him—or because they don't like the car he drives or the way he looks. If they only knew what some of those kids at church are really like—the ones they think are so goody-goody—they wouldn't be so all-fired happy to have me run around with them either. There are some really great con artists among those church kids. At least my friends are honest."

I suppose I've had that particular conversation with young people a few hundred times.

Why Him — or Her?

Why not ask your son or daughter what it is he or she likes about a certain friend. A teenager may find it hard to articulate a friend's qualities, but eventually, if you persist, you'll find out what makes the friendship work. Sometimes it'll be something like "She likes me."

An awful lot of what adolescence is all about is finding a comfort zone — finding some peer group that will "accept me." Remember the story of Esau who sold his birthright for a mess of pottage? Well, most adolescents would sell their birthrights for what may look to you like a mess of pottage. At a certain stage, the acceptance of a peer will mean a hundred times more to them than the acceptance of a parent.

Teenagers face a lot of rejection in high school, and that one person may simply be willing to spend time with your son or daughter. When you don't have an awful lot of friendship offered, someone who is simply there is of great value. Before you discount this as a positive quality, think it through. Being friendless means being lonely. You feel as if there must be something wrong with you. To have someone who offers his or her presence or, more, something that feels like loyalty is very important to your son or daughter.

This is often the bottom line for teenage friendships: "For some reason this person is willing to hang around with me. Even more, this kid sticks with me through thick or thin — we're friends." If you pursue further, you may find that this has another dimension. This person is willing to listen to your teenager. There is an awesome power in the listening ear. A young person desperately wants to have someone who will listen to problems, listen to opinions, viewpoints, dreams, angers, frustrations, hopes, and fears. No doubt this friend not only listens but does so uncritically. That is, he or she doesn't put value and judgment on what your son or daughter says. "This person is still my friend even though I tell her the truth and even though I tell her how I feel. She doesn't reject me or tell me I'm bad. She simply listens to me and attempts to identify with my feelings."

In every teenage community there are in-groups and out-groups. There are kids who are accepted and are part of the organized structure, and there are kids who don't feel they fit in. If you hang around the local 7-Eleven or wherever those who don't fit in gather, you'll find that they usually have their own code, their own standards, and their own loyalties. Often, these standards of conduct are very high. In fact, they spend a lot of time keeping track of the other groups in school, noticing how unaccepting, unloving, and judgmental they are. They take quite a lot of pride in not judging people by the way they look. In this "out-group" you may find the pudgy girls, the boys with bad complexions, the unathletic, the kids who have had trouble in the past and have gotten over it, the kids who started out slow in school, the kids whose families have moved a lot. The kids in this group generally have some pretty positive characteristics about them, and they tend to find one another.

When your own teenager makes friends in a group like this, he or she may resist giving up the peer group just because they use alcohol or take drugs or have taken drugs or are suspected of stealing. "But they haven't stolen from me. Their behavior hasn't hurt me. They're my friends." Let's face it — a bird in the hand is worth two in the bush, especially when those seem to be your only options.

I realize when a bedraggled, uncommunicative kid walks into your house behind your teenager, it's a little hard to say, "Let's see, what do we have here? We have someone who is willing to be available to my teenager. Someone who is willing to be loyal, willing to listen, willing to be uncritical and accepting, and willing to accept my son or daughter unconditionally." But that just might be what you have. When you put those attributes in one person, even if he or she is wearing a frayed military jacket or has purple hair, they are pretty attractive. Many people would consider themselves fortunate if sometime in their lives they had even one person who would give to them what this young person gives your teen.

If your son has a friend who is giving what I've described, or any small measure of it, it's no wonder he feels threatened and unhappy if you suggest giving up that person. Indeed, such a friend is a rare find, even if that person looks undesirable to you.

> *Attitudes toward our teenager's friends are as important as our actions.* Teenagers tend to be intensely loyal. To disparage a friend is to insult your teen. We should think twice before we dispense criticisms of our adolescents' friends. Even when we have some serious questions about our adolescents' friends, it is best to refrain from criticism. Instead, we can ask our adolescents how *they* feel about the friend in question. Quite often you will find your son or daughter has some of the same reservations you do. If we take time to listen and don't jump in too soon, we may find that they are pretty good judges of character themselves!

> If our teenagers don't perceive some potential problem that we observe, we can raise our concern in a nonjudgmental way. We might say, "What do you think about Tom's drinking?" Or "I wonder why Tom has trouble getting along with his teachers?" These questions or other concerned comments express concern over Tom's well-being. They also encourage discussion that is instantly canceled by accusatory statements like: "I don't want you running around with that alcoholic!" or, "Your friend has a terrible attitude!"[1]

Come on In

What can you do to help overcome your parental misgivings about the "wrong friends"? Try inviting them into your own home. It's not always pleasant to have young people underfoot, yet I've always felt it's better to have an open home than to have them — your children *and* their friends — hanging around someone else's home where the standards may not be as high or where there may be no adult supervision.

Janie and I have always keenly felt that we should not be simply absorbing our environment. Rather, we should be influencing those around us. I'm on the air on about four hundred radio stations five times a week, and from those broadcasts I receive a considerable amount of mail. A great number of those letters ask, "How can I keep my young person from being influenced by the bad element at school, the wrong kind of kids?"

I always find this question curious in light of 1 John 4:4: "Greater is He that is in you, than he that is in the world."

A person or a family who follows Christ, who is filled with the Holy Spirit, ought to have a Power within that's stronger than the powers of this world. A strong, loving family, with parents who truly are concerned about their children, can provide an atmosphere in which young people who have not been taught respect, who have not been taught right from wrong, who have lived pretty much a mirror reflection of this culture, can be positively influenced. As we have opened our home and let outsiders be a part of our family life, we have trusted that in all of it we would be witnesses for Christ.

(One related point I'd like to make here: Many young people who have come into our home with our children have wanted to call me Uncle Jay or sometimes even Dad. Some have called me Uncle, but I've never encouraged them to call me Dad. Unless a young person is actually parentless, I feel that title should be reserved for one's own father. I've never wanted to drive a wedge between a young person and his or her parent. In fact, I always work hard to try to find some good attributes in a parent and constantly point them out to a young person to affirm and build the parent-child relationship.)

Ultimately, we've found that a great many of these "adopted" young people have attempted to make their own adult homes like our own. They've wanted us to come to their weddings. They've brought their children around for us to see. They've sought out our approval. Perhaps they sensed our willingness to give affirmation and show some interest in them. The point, however, is that we've always tried to help influence our children's friends to become the kind of persons that we want them to be. We have rejoiced as some have come to Christ and we've watched them grow as Christians, marry other Christians, and start to raise their own children in the faith. We have seen other parents "catch" this positive-influence attitude and have seen it work in other homes as well as our own.

Accepting People, Rejecting Behavior

What about your teen's friends whose undue negative influence isn't tolerable—for instance a boy who is unwilling to show respect for your daughter? Well, you need to sit down with your teen and, rather than attack the individual, talk about the behavior that you will not countenance.

As I've studied the New Testament, I've found God rejecting not persons but certain behaviors. Christ always encourages people to come to God and welcomes them when they arrive. In fact, Jesus was criticized on this exact point. The Pharisees, thinking they could purify the world by rejecting certain kinds of people, criticized Jesus for spending time with sinners. In this context, Jesus said, "They that be whole need not a physician, but they that are sick" (Matthew 9:12). His words sound so sensible. Of course a person who is needy needs more attention than the person who is functioning well.

But despite what we know in our heads, despite all the Bible studies and all the sermons, many of us still find it difficult to apply this principle close to home, when it comes to the friends of our own children. It's not easy to take an unlikable young person on a family vacation or to have that teen underfoot all the time. But that situation is far better than driving a wedge between you and your own child because you have refused to let your child make judgments about friends.

I'm Doing the Best I Can

At the base of it, what kids resent most is the feeling that they are not trusted, as we have already pointed out in a previous chapter. "My parents won't even trust me to choose my own friends. I know what's right and wrong, and even if this friend does things that aren't right, I don't do those things. I can be with kids who are doing wrong and still do right. Why do they insist that I'm such a baby and they've got to protect me from other people? If they only knew how many times I say no to wrong things. If they only knew how much I stand up for right — and stand up for God and stand up for them and stand up for our home and stand up for our values — they'd trust me. They don't bother to find out that I spend a lot of time doing this. They're just afraid that I'll get into trouble and embarrass them."

The following letter from a teenager pleads for this understanding:

> I wish that my parents understood I am a sexual being. Even though I am not married or even seriously involved with anyone right now, I still have sexual urges. My parents have difficulty understanding this because they believe that those kind of emotions should only come with commitment. Although I believe that these urges should not be indulged in until marriage, I can't help it when they come upon me. Try as I may, they seem to creep into my mind and body when they will. I wish my parents understood that I do hold the same convictions that they do about having sex before marriage and that I am trying to control my sexual thoughts and urges, but it isn't easy, and I need support to keep from giving in to them.[2]

I remember counseling a young man whose father was concerned because his son's friends who were always hanging around the house all seemed to be effeminate; the father was afraid the boy was getting involved with homosexuals. When I confronted the issue, the son said, "Why, of course they're homosexuals. I know they are. I'm not; they are. But these guys have been rejected by the church. If everybody rejects them, then how in the world are they going to be saved? I've just been trying to tell them that they don't need to live this way, that they can live for Christ. You've got to trust me. I know what I'm doing. I'm not going to get in trouble."

I then spent some time trying to explain to this handsome, athletic young man that these friends could be trying to seduce him. And I further explained that his father had seen him lounging around on a summer afternoon with these guys in gym shorts and tank tops. That scene is what had frightened the father.

The boy said, "Really? I never thought about that."

I commented, "You know how you can be aroused around women?"

He said, "Yeah, my girlfriend and I, we can just be sitting, drinking a soda, and I get all aroused. It's kind of embarrassing if you don't have control over those things."

I continued, "Well, these young men may have a similar reaction when they're in that situation with you."

At his suggestion, we agreed that he'd start being more careful.

Some months later we talked about it again. "How are those friendships going?" I asked.

"Well," he said, "those guys have quit hanging around. They've kind of given up on me."

"Why do you suppose that is?" I asked.

And he said, "Well, I think maybe they knew how much I wanted them to come to know Christ. They sensed I was willing to be their friend but that I wouldn't join their lifestyle. I think once they knew that, they weren't as interested in me as they were before."

I was very proud of that young man. I think it takes a great deal of courage to attempt to be a witness for Christ across such difficult barriers. He maintained a strong witness, but, in this case, I believe he learned something about the complexity of life and relationships. Though his motivations are still good, and though he might try the same process again, he'll be more wary next time, having discovered that people's motives are not always what they seem. But, he had been permitted to reach some of those conclusions, with guidance, by his own discernment.

Setting Limits

In situations involving drugs, alcohol, and other potentially dangerous things we must sit our children down and draw the lines. Let's say your daughter's friend has a drinking problem. You might say, "If you're going to be a friend to this girl, then I'm going to insist that you not ride in a car that she's driving if she's had anything to drink. Either you can drive and take responsibility, or you call home and we'll come and get you."

One night one of our daughters came home from a party very early in the evening. "How come you're home so soon?" I asked. "The party can't be over already." At that, she burst into tears.

"What's wrong, honey? Why are you crying?"

"Oh, it just seems like I can never have any fun."

"What do you mean—no fun?"

"Well, I went to this party and before long everybody started drinking, so I just told them to bring me home and now I'm home all alone and I'm not having any fun."

I had to think quickly. "Well, would you like to be at a party like that, where everybody's drinking and carrying on?"

"No, not really, Dad. It's just that I get kind of tired of being alone."

We sat there on the edge of the bed and talked for quite a long while. It was truly a golden moment in my relationship with her as I expressed how very proud I was of her, how much I loved her, how much I wished we could have some fun together as a family; maybe we could do something to make up for her unhappiness. I don't remember now what we did—maybe nothing more than commiserating and talking about the cost of discipleship—but I do know that I was very comforted to know that my daughter had the sense to say "I want to go home" when she felt she should.

Don't make the mistake of saying, "I don't want you hanging around with those kids," until, first, you've made an effort to understand who "those kids" are and why your teenager wants to be with them; and, second, you've looked for a way to be redemptive in their lives.

Every human being has either a positive or a negative charge. That is, we all tend to make the two or three feet around us more like ourselves, or we tend to absorb the two or three feet around us. If our teen is the kind of person who absorbs the two or three feet around him, it's very dangerous for him to be around anybody who has negative habits or behavior. By the same token, if our teen is the kind of person who's influencing those around him; if she's assertive in her lifestyle and witness; if he's not absorbing an environment but creating one, then we can feel comfortable knowing that they can go into the highways and byways of life and inspire others. They can help the sick become well and make those who are away from God see the light of the Gospel.

FAILURE TO GIVE YOUR TEENAGER THE RIGHT TO FAIL

"You Did What?"

There is no message that takes up as much New Testament space as that of grace. At times it seems that Paul is obsessed with the idea: "For by grace are ye saved through faith; and that not of yourselves: it is a gift of God: not of works, lest any man should boast" (Ephesians 2:8-9). But Paul's concern with grace rarely reaches into our homes. It seems the enemy of our souls (and ultimately the enemy of our families and our relationships) succeeds in no attack so well as the attack against grace.

While we know intellectually that we're saved by grace, that Jesus is a friend of sinners, that we all come short of the glory of God, that no one is righteous, we persist in the idea that God accepts us only if we are perfect. Years ago, Dick Halverson, now Chaplain of the United States Senate, made a comment that has become one of several anchor points of my Christian understanding. He said, "There is nothing you can do to make God love you more and nothing you can do to make God love you less." What a beautiful definition of grace!

God's love is unconditional—not based on performance. And yet we gradually internalize the idea that we are loved more if we are good than if we're bad.

As a child I was fortunate; I always felt loved. I never doubted that my parents cared for me—supremely. On the other hand, I somehow heard the message wrong. I heard, "We'll love you *more* if you're a good boy than if you're a bad boy. We'll love you *more* if you get good grades than if you get bad grades. We'll love you *more* if you bring honor on this family than if you bring dishonor." Now I know what was really being said was, "We would be pleased if you'd get good grades. We would be pleased if you'd be a good boy. We would be pleased if you would bring honor on this family." But being pleased and being loved got confused in my mind. I had attached performance to love, and I felt that there was something wrong with me because I could never reach a perfect standard. I always knew about my shortcomings, and so I spent much of my life dwelling on them.

I thought this was my own unique problem until I began to minister the Gospel, especially among young people. I then saw that the overwhelming majority of people have connected performance with love. Most of us somehow view love as being conditioned upon accomplishment.

There's probably no mistake more fatal in the parent-teen relationship than communicating the idea that one cannot fail, and that if one does fail he or she is reduced to starting all over again. There's no residue of built-up virtue or any value to the person; it has all been blown in one fell swoop.

A while back I held extended meetings in a church, and after services at night I was entertained in various homes. The current rage then was the game called Aggravation. It's a board game, something like Sorry, but played with marbles. You move your marbles around the edge of the board, and though I don't remember all the rules, I clearly remember you could spend the entire evening slowly moving around the whole board only to have someone pounce on you and make you go back to the starting line. Believe me, Aggravation was aggravating. Though there was always a great deal of laughter when someone had to move back to the beginning, the frustration was incredible.

Too often, this is what happens to a teenager. "I could live my life as a good person, I could be a dutiful daughter, but then as soon as I make a single mistake, all the trust my parents have had in me is wiped away. The slate is completely erased, and I've got to start out as if I'm a baby again, winning trust a little bit at a time."

Young people raised with this sense of aggravation will often withdraw, pull into themselves, and become afraid to compete in anything, maybe for the rest of their lives. They have what I call the mentality of the 100 percenter. That is, 100 percent is success. Anything less than 100 percent is failure. It's a kind of perfectionism that has a way of destroying and defeating the soul.

People often write to me and ask, "Why does my son lie all the time?" This is a complex question. Sometimes it's because kids feel their lives are not very important. As they see it, because their "real world" is something no one would be interested in, they fabricate a fantasy world that makes them seem important and successful. Other times young people lie because they want to weasel out of responsibility. But very often young people lie because those they're dealing with, usually parents, have set up such a standard of perfection that it's better to take the risk of deception than to admit failure and face the consequences of being reduced to ground zero once again.

I doubt that there's a salesman in the land who's escaped the motivational seminar in which someone sets down a glass half filled with water. The leader then asks the participants to describe the glass. Some write that they see a glass half filled with water and others that they see a glass half empty. Then those who see the glass as being half empty are told that they have a pessimistic spirit, not looking at the world with enthusiasm and optimism. I'm not sure this illustration is foolproof, but I do know that the parent who makes the mistake of not allowing his or her young person the freedom to fail, who makes the young person return to square one, who does not understand the importance of the application of grace in a family, will develop that negative spirit in that child.

Having directed a large organization employing hundreds of young men and women in youth work, I will assure you that this perfectionism is one of the most debilitating things that can happen to a person both theologically and in terms of being able to accomplish goals and aggressively serve the Lord. With no understanding of the grace of God, these people are defeated spiritually, for when they fail, they can't get up, confess their sin, and move ahead with any assurance that God's hand is on them. They feel condemned even though Jesus Christ has died for them. In a sense, it's as if Jesus has died in vain. Though they are forgiven by God, though they are forgiven by their neighbors, they can't forgive themselves because someone has built in them the idea that unless you're a 100 percenter, unless you succeed all the time, you're a miserable failure. As a result, they can't follow God with enthusiasm and take on great exploits for His Kingdom.

We must not let lack of perfection hold us back; we must not be afraid and timid to do the will of God. But we must understand that when we try to do the will of God and fail, our Heavenly Father looks down and remembers that we're dust.

God Knows Our Frame

Nothing is more opposite of the spirit of the New Testament than the spirit of perfectionism. When it comes to the nature of mankind, the Bible is a very realistic book. In fact, one of the most beautiful phrases in all the Bible is the psalmist's "He knows our frame; He remembers that we are dust" (Psalm 103:14 NKJV). To me this says that God knows well the limitations of mankind. As David further said, "It is he that hath made us, and not we ourselves" (Psalm 100:3). That is, we are the creations of God.

He's the Creator; we're the created. He's the Infinite; we're the finite. He is the Superior; we're the inferior. And He takes responsibility for what He's created. He has made us in His image. He has given us the ability to choose our destiny. He has given us a will that allows us to rebel or be obedient. But God understands us and looks down on us, as the Scripture says, "As a father pitieth his children" (Psalm 103:13). With a compassionate heart He looks down on us and our limitations, much as we would look at a small child who is fumblingly trying to act like an adult.

Janie and I are grandparents now, and I keenly remember the evening one of our grandsons welcomed his new brother into his home. He came up to the baby, who was getting all the attention, and tried to express his love and interest. But as a toddler, his motor coordination wasn't all that good, so when he tried to touch or pat the baby he'd bring his hand down in almost a slap, making the baby wince or blink. He'd stick his finger in the baby's eye, not maliciously but simply in a typical two-year-old, clumsy attempt to show love toward a newborn brother.

I often think that we must look a lot like that to a loving God. Though He wants to restrain us from doing the wrongs we do, He knows our motives and He knows that we sometimes do these things simply because we are ignorant, limited, and immature. Romans 8:29 says that we are eventually to be conformed to the image of God's Son. Apparently this is a process, not something that happens immediately.

Many sects within the Christian faith have sought immediate perfection by kneeling at an altar or speaking a certain kind of prayer or performing a certain kind of ritual. These Christians desire God, in one great gesture, to bestow a sanctification and perfection that will last the rest of his or her life. Though many people would like to achieve such perfection, it simply doesn't happen that way.

A parent's relationship with his or her children is not unlike our relationship with God. Our children are fumblingly and stumblingly finding their way into maturity. Many of the mistakes they make are the mistakes of ineptitude, of lack of foresight, of poor judgment, of impatience. Immature people do those things. Our children are, after all, adolescents. If they acted in a mature fashion, had long-range goals before them at all times, made mature decisions every time they were faced with a dilemma, then we wouldn't call them children or adolescents; we'd call them adults.

Immature people obviously cannot achieve adult levels of performance and will doubtlessly fail many times before they succeed. It is very important that parents understand this growth process and understand that young people have not yet attained it.

The apostle Paul spoke about this in his own life. To the Philippian Christians he expressed his present state of imperfection. He said, "I press toward the mark of the prize of the high calling of God in Christ Jesus" (Philippians 3:14). Let me paraphrase that as, "I count not myself to have apprehended or to have attained, but I press toward the mark." Even when we fail there can be a smile on the face of God and a pat on our shoulder that says, "Well done, good and faithful servant." Why? Because our God knows our hearts and He knows who and where we are. Through the blood of His Son, He sees us separate from our sin.

There's More to a Doughnut Than a Hole

One day I was invited to a home where a son had been accused by a schoolmate's mother of stealing the schoolmate's motor bike. The accused boy claimed that he had traded the bike for a ball glove. That story didn't make any sense to either mother, especially the one who'd called the police. "That's ridiculous," she said, "A ball glove doesn't have 5 percent the value of a motorbike. He's lying. He's stolen my son's motor bike."

Well, the accused's mother was distraught, believing she had a thief on her hands. I said, "Well, first of all, you've got to understand that twelve-year-old boys will often trade things without any regard to their value." When a boy wants something badly enough, he'll make a bad bargain, especially if it was something given to him, not something he actually had to work to pay for. "Easy come, easy go" is the way many young people think. So I said, "I wouldn't discount the story out of hand because it is just nutty enough to sound like something a boy that age would do. But second, even if he did steal it, I don't think you should think of your boy as a thief." I then went on to explain that an eleven-year-old boy has lived about four thousand days. So if a boy steals a bicycle on one day, why would you totally discount the 3,999 good days up to that point? It's like a doughnut. A doughnut isn't all hole; there's something around the edge. A boy who tells a lie is just that; he's a boy who has told a lie — not a liar.

A fellow who used to attend our church got an award for being an outstanding Illinois state trooper. I was so proud of him, and when I congratulated him, I said, "Jim, the governor said that your fifteen-year file didn't show one case of your having roughed up a drunk or used excessive force. In fifteen years as a state trooper, out on the street, how did you manage such a record?"

Now, Jim's a shy guy, and I had to drag an answer out of him. But finally he said, "Well, Jay, two things. Number one, say I'm called to handle a group of guys who are causing a disturbance in a tavern. I never say to myself, *There's a drunk.* I always say, *There's a man — someone's husband, someone's father, someone's son, someone's neighbor — who got drunk.* So I always try to think of him as a man, not as a crime. And second, the Bible says that a soft answer turns away wrath. Whenever I walk up to the window of an automobile, no matter what voice someone speaks in, I always speak a little lower. I don't know if it's anything special, but it's just worked for fifteen years."

Your boy may be absolutely frustrating, but he's still a boy — your boy. He may have done something that embarrasses you to death, but he is not *that*, he is a boy who did something that embarrassed you.

Even though on this particular day your son or daughter may have failed miserably — perhaps something as serious as stealing a motor bike. Or perhaps your daughter has, on one careless evening, become pregnant. Don't let that one failure, no matter how great it might seem, wipe out all the times that child said no to temptation, all the times he or she said yes to God, all the days he or she dutifully loved you and the Lord.

An Example of Grace

A friend of mine, Don Lonie, dean of youth communicators, once told me about a decision he had made with his teenagers, and I think it's a beautiful idea.

One day his son came home, obviously upset. "Dad," he said, "I've had an accident and I've dented in the front end of the car. How can I ever repay you? I'm so sorry. I bet our insurance rates will go up."

Don said, "Well, yes, it is serious. But are you all right?"

"Yes."

"Are the other people all right?"

"Yes."

"Well, it's simply tin, and it can be pounded out and repainted. In fact, here's what I'll do. We have a deductible insurance policy, and a long time ago, when you were a little boy, I decided that I was going to pay the deductible on your first fender bender. Only the first one. After this, the grace period's over and you'll have to pay. But all of us do foolish things when we drive. I've had accidents myself and so has your mother and virtually every other driver in the world. But in order for you to understand how grace works, I want you to know I'm going to pay this."

The son just stood there, stared at Don, then began to cry. "Dad, thank you so much."

Wanting to make sure he understood, Don said, "Now this isn't about money. It's not about the deductible. It's about the grace of God."

Don did the same thing when his daughter got her first traffic ticket. She came home, embarrassed, and said, "Dad, I stopped for going forty in a thirty-mile zone"—or running a stop light or whatever it was that she had done.

Don said, "Honey, when you were a little girl I made a vow that I was going to pay the first traffic violation for each of you kids, because there's not a dad in the world who hasn't looked out of his rearview mirror and seen that flashing light that says 'pull over.' You've done something wrong, maybe even inadvertently, and you've been caught. I know what it feels like. I've been there. So this time I'm going to pay your traffic ticket because I want you to know how grace works and operates."

I picked up this idea and practiced it with my own children. It's one of the best ways I can imagine of helping a young person understand that he or she doesn't always have to be perfect.

Stand by Me

Having worked with the juvenile justice system, I've often wondered why one boy goes straight after one brush with the law and another eventually ends up in a juvenile detention center or prison. One difference I have identified has to do with parental attitudes. The boy with a father who would go with him, stand in the courtroom with him, face the judge with him, and accept dual responsibility was generally able to pull out of the problem, find redemption, and make a contribution to society. But the kids who are in jail and in constant trouble with the law are kids who do not have parents who will stand with them. They say instead, "I will claim only a perfect boy—a perfect girl. And if they're not perfect, I don't want anything to do with them."

It is a tragic mistake not to give our young people the right to fail, because it's through their failure that we can show our love—as God through our failure shows us His love. It's through their failure that we can help them understand the forgiveness of God, and it's through showing grace toward them that we can teach them this repeated message of the New Testament — the message of the grace of God.

In his book *But You Don't Understand*, Paul Borthwick says:

> Talking of forgiveness and mercy like this makes many Christian parents quite nervous because they fear that they will become too permissive, never disciplining their children. This is a mistaken concept of mercy that should be corrected.
>
> Admitting that you fail, forgiving and forgetting, and releasing your past do not mean that you give your teenagers free license to sin and break your rules and God's rules. If *mercy* is defined as "giving someone what he needs, not what he deserves," there is plenty of room for forgiveness in the context of stern discipline. Teenagers need to know that breaking the rules has consequences. Forgiving and covering up consequences could be a big mistake for parents.
>
> The mistakes of youth are to be expected, but these mistakes can be valuable learning experiences if handled correctly. To do this, however, consider these responses:
>
> • When your teenager sins, forgive him from the heart.
>
> • In dealing with the sin, consider the response.
>
> • If the teen is repentant, take this into consideration in your discipline. If the teen is rebellious, you might need to be more severe.
>
> • If there is to be a penalty (maybe the confession is penalty enough), make sure it fits the crime: in other words, grounding the teen for the summer for failing to take out the trash would be too severe.
>
> • Make sure your emotions are under control, for "the wrath of man does not produce the righteousness of God" (James 1:20). If they are not, wait before dealing with your teen's problem.

- After forgiveness and penalty (if any), let your teen know that your love is unchanged. Be willing to forget the sin and not bring it up again. One parent suggests a hug or a verbal "I love you" after the penalty is over.

Forgiveness and discipline are not mutually exclusive. Instead, they should go hand in hand with growth and learning from mistakes. The toughest assignment of the parent will always be determining how to communicate best both the mercy of God and the discipline of the Spirit to the growing teenager.[1]

TEN

FAILURE TO DISCUSS THE UNCOMFORTABLE

"Do You Mind If We Talk about Something Else?"

Some issues are simply difficult to discuss with one's children. Sex, drugs, masturbation, physiological changes (such as menstrual cycles), the death of a friend or relative, and divorce are all issues that are easier to avoid than to confront head on. But with or without parental help, teens *will* deal with these issues.

If Christian parents don't talk about the uncomfortable in a sensitive, direct but matter-of-fact way, teens will find answers on their own. Generally, the results of that route are unacceptable to all parties. Parental involvement is becoming increasingly important, as young people today come in contact with so many of life's experiences that once were discussed only in very discreet circles.

Most any evening a young person watching television can hear references or innuendoes describing adultery and homosexuality. Television comedians commonly allude to sexual issues in ways that are suggestive and bring up questions in young minds. Images on the screen evoke curiosity. One does not have to attend R- or X-rated movies to see them. Many young people from Christian homes have seen more R-rated movies than we'd like to admit. They have seen and heard allusions to virtually every possible human experience, and usually in a context that treats sin as simply an alternate lifestyle or perhaps even something that is attractive — something one may want to do. The rule of the day seems to be, "Different strokes for different folks." And that pervasive attitude puts today's parents at a real disadvantage.

Because of this, it is important for parents to begin to discuss the realities of life with young people as soon as they are ready and surely by the time they are teenagers. Young people run into issues of sexuality, drugs, alcohol, divorce, somewhere: in the schoolroom, in the locker room, in conversations with other teenagers, at camp, in a book or movie. It's important to openly discuss these things with teenagers so that your children can take advantage of your own insight into these struggles. It also keeps them from holding you in contempt because they think you are too ignorant to deal with real problems.

Information Please

It's amazing to me how many kids don't think that their parents have a sex life. They know that Jesus was born of a virgin, and they suspect that maybe they were too. They tend to look at their parents and say, "Mother would never do that." They see her in so many prim and prescribed and proper settings that they can't believe mother possesses any passion at all. If she and Dad did manage to conceive one or more children, then that was the extent of their sex life. They surely can't be enjoying a on-going sexual relationship. I have felt that it's important to begin discussions about sex with our kids so that we can share together our human experience and its relationship to faith.

Christian education actually belongs in the home. And part of the responsibility of Christian education is to have these kinds of conversations. The church can't be expected to fulfill parental responsibility. In a few hours a week relative strangers can't be expected to do what we are charged to do 168 hours a week. I see these responsibilities and privileges as being at least as important as meeting the physical needs of food, clothing, and shelter.

When it comes to the issue of sex, children first need basic information from their parents. In his book *What I Wish My Parents Knew about My Sexuality,* evangelist Josh McDowell points this out:

A poll of 1,000 teenagers revealed that sex information was gained in the following ways:

(A) Only 32 percent of the girls and 15 percent of the boys were informed about sex by their parents.

(B) 53 percent of the boys and 42 percent of the girls found out from friends their own age.

(C) 15 percent piece together the information they had received from other sources.

(D) 56 percent of these young people acquire their sex knowledge between the sixth and ninth grades and 18 percent learned about sex before the fifth grade.

(E) A full 88 percent of these young people felt they needed more information about sex than they had received from their parents.

In connection with those poll results, McDowell prints a letter from a teenager:

Virginity and the sacredness of sex is something all teenagers should be informed of. My Christian high school does not offer sex education classes and feels it is the responsibility of parents to inform the children. What if parents fail to take on this responsibility? Teenagers are curious, and their ignorance, due to lack of adult responsibility, might get them mixed up in premarital sex. The teenager is responsible for his or her actions, but is it entirely the fault of the teenager since they were not informed of the dangers of premarital sex? It is not.

Partial responsibility must be laid on those who neglected to inform the teenagers.

The only thing kids know are what they learn in locker rooms and school halls. Parents won't teach their children about sex at home, so they learn the hard way — at school and on the streets. In their hearts, teenagers who engage in premarital sex usually blame their parents. To an extent it is the parents' fault because of the failure to be open with their children on the subject of sex. Instead, parents turn them off and change the subject. When parents turn away from the subject, teens are all the more curious to learn about it — even on their own.[1]

In our particular case, it did not ever seem right to sit down and simply say, "Let's talk about the facts of life." When each of our children reached about eleven years old, I gave them a series of records on sex and asked them to listen to them. Then we listened to them together and discussed them. The person on the record talked about human sexuality in clinical terms, explaining bodily parts and what it was all about.

We found that our kids were quite embarrassed and didn't seem ready for this approach. After we went through the exercise one time, we gave up the idea because it just didn't seem right.

We then decided to use Jesus' method of teaching. He walked through the land and dealt with particular situations and problems as He ran into them. That is, the world around Him set His agenda.

Taking this approach with our children worked something like this: We would be watching television, and something would be said that prompted gales of canned laughter. At that point I asked, "What did he say?"

One of the kids would answer, "He said such-and-such."

Then I would say, "Do you know what that means." And a discussion started. Sometimes I would say, "How would you feel if Daddy were to do that particular thing? How would you feel if Mother were to do that?"

The kids would say, "That would be awful. Nobody ought to do that."

I'd say, "I wonder why they laughed about it then?" The television was often the jumping-off place for the discussion of these difficult issues.

Sometimes, I've learned, the time to speak up is when you least feel like it. When the kids were young teens, say, freshmen in high school or eighth graders, we would be watching television when suddenly the room would get stone quiet. The kids wouldn't even blink; they were so embarrassed about what they'd just seen or heard. At that point I always wanted to clear my throat and go to the refrigerator to find something to eat or drink. I'd have to force myself to stay and say, "What are they doing?" or, "Why are they doing that?" The question might be, "Do you think that would be a good thing for us to do? Are we watching something here that would be bad if we did it? Does this mean we should stop watching this program?

When this happens at your house, stop and analyze the situation. See it for what it really is.

As our daughters began to face their growth into womanhood, Janie sat down with them and discussed what was happening in their bodies. As our son began to grow into manhood, I discussed similar issues with him.

Keeping the Channels Open

As embarrassing as the subject is for you and for your son or daughter, sexuality is too important an issue to ignore.

Dr. Bruce Narramore frankly states:

Unfortunately, many parents have not felt sufficiently comfortable with their own sexuality to talk freely about their body functions and prepare their daughters emotionally for menstruation. Astonishing numbers of girls receive no explanation of even basic sexual functions. They meet the onset of menstruation with distress and confusion, wondering what is wrong and what, if anything, can be done to overcome this "problem." As one girl put it, "My mother talked about my period like the plague!"

Masturbation is an almost universal practice among teenage boys and, although the statistics are less complete, a common experience among teen girls. Approximately 90 percent of teenage boys surveyed acknowledge masturbating, at least occasionally. About half as many girls engage in masturbation, according to John Conger in *Contemporary Issues in Adolescent Development* (Harper & Row). This form of sexual experimentation can stimulate a great deal of anxiety and guilt, if the adolescent is unprepared. He wonders if masturbation is normal. He wonders if it is morally wrong. And he wonders what his parents would think or say if they knew about his secret activities. The cycle of stimulation, secrecy, fear, and guilt can become a real problem for the teenager who is already prone to excessive feelings of anxiety and guilt.

Sexually oriented jokes, girlie magazines, and the recounting of sexual adventures appeal strongly to many adolescents, but innate modesty and anxiety toward the unknown cause a simultaneous hesitation. The conflict heightens for the Christian teenager with definite moral scruples. He yearns to satisfy his curiosity and to still live up to his ideals.

When parents have been factual and natural about their bodies, children's adaptation to sexual development will proceed smoothly. No undue curiosity about sex will dominate their minds, and a deep respect for their bodies will protect them from abusing this gift.[2]

It's not enough to explain to girls the wonders of their own bodies, and to boys, the wonders of their own gender. The fewer surprises your adolescent encounters, the better he or she will be able to handle new and awkward situations.

Suppose a group of teens is at the lake cottage on a hot afternoon sitting around in their bathing suits, jumping in and out of the boat, water skiing. Temptation will surface. Daughters need to have this explained to them. So do sons. They need to understand that a male's sexual trigger is in the mind's eye. What he sees — or what he thinks he sees — turns him on, and quickly. It is intense, and it comes and goes. Female sexual response is much less visual and slower. It has more to do with what she thinks and/or feels — her thoughts of security, happiness, being with this person, and of a long-range, intense relationship. So in an innocent, frolicking afternoon at the lake, she can be approached by a boy in ways that baffle her. It doesn't mean he's a bad boy; it means he's male and she's female. A wise mother sits a daughter down and explains this to her. A wise father tells his son how to understand these temptations and how a dip in the cold lake will often be of greater value than any amount of conversation. He needs to learn to sublimate his desires and be active — not just slouch around, drink diet colas, and look at her body.

One cannot have a once-and-for-all conversation about sexuality — or drugs or death. As you pray, ask the Holy Spirit's guidance and help to allow you to see opportunities. If you have an open and natural attitude, they might come more than you expect.

I remember one Sunday in particular. On the way to church my son said to me, "Dad, I'm embarrassed."

"About what?" I asked.

"Well, a friend and I went to a movie last night that wasn't very good."

"What movie was it?"

He said, "Well, it was a porno flick."

I was worried. *My goodness, what has he seen?* I thought. Well I found out it wasn't actually an X-rated porno flick; it was a film playing in all of the local theaters about a troubled young woman who felt very insecure and unlovely. As a result, she threw herself at men, hoping to be reassured of her loveliness. Men preyed upon her and used her until eventually she was killed by a madman in a lustful rage.

I said, "Well, what makes you feel embarrassed this morning?"

"First of all, I'm embarrassed to be a man because of the way these men acted in this film. They acted like slobbering animals, rather than like human beings. They treated women as if they were just things. Objects. It turned everything that God made, everything that's supposed to be beautiful, into something very ugly."

The more he talked, the more proud I was of him. I realized that somehow through all those years of training at home, through all our family relationships, through the Sunday school, through youth group, through the Campus Life Club, he had developed character enough to discern when he was in an atmosphere that was ugly and wrong and out of harmony with God's creation. Though we were talking about something in which he felt a certain sense of shame, I felt that God was showing me that my son had begun to understand the nature of God's creation — male and female as God understood it. God gave him a beautiful image of what he and his marriage could be. Bruce was holding onto that rather than to what the media was trying to make sex out to be.

Find Out What's Hot

Whenever specific things come up, sometimes during crises and difficulties, talk about them. In every church, parents of senior-high kids and of junior-high kids ought to meet together in respective groups two to four times a year to discuss what their kids are facing. What problems are coming up? What are the kids talking about? Any new information gained in those meetings can then become discussion-starters back home. The same kind of what's-hot answers can be found by reading the school paper and attending school events — watching the behavior of teens.

As things happen at school, as classmates get pregnant, as boys have to leave school and get married, as young people get in trouble with drugs, talk about it.

If a subject comes up that you need more information to discuss, do some homework. For instance, you may need to know what the symptoms of drug abuse are. In his bestseller *Dare to Discipline,* James Dobson gives eight possible signals:

1. Inflammation of the eyelids and nose is common. The pupils of the eyes are either very wide or very small, depending on the kind of drugs internalized.

2. The extremes of energy may be represented. Either the individual is sluggish, gloomy, and withdrawn, or he may be loud, hysterical, and jumpy.

3. The appetite is extreme—either very great or very poor. Weight loss may occur.

4. The personality suddenly changes; the individual may become irritable, inattentive, and confused, or aggressive, suspicious, and explosive.

5. Body and breath odor is often bad. Cleanliness is generally ignored.

6. The digestive system may be upset—diarrhea, nausea, and vomiting may occur. Headaches and double vision are also common. Other signs of physical deterioration may include change in skin tone and body stance.

7. Needle marks on the body, usually appearing on the arms, are an important symptom. These punctures sometimes get infected and appear as sores and boils.

8. Moral values often crumble and are replaced by new, way-out ideas and values.

Each drug produces its own unique symptoms; thus, the above list is not specific to a particular substance. If the parent suspects that his teenager is using narcotics or dangerous drugs, it is suggested that the family physician be consulted immediately.[3]

If young men get kicked off the basketball team or someone gets suspended from school for using drugs or alcohol, pick up on it. Sit down and discuss these issues—maybe at dinner. Over the years we insisted that the family eat the evening meal together. And we tried not to simply grab our food and head for the television set. We sat at the table and talked to one another, especially about issues that touched the kids' lives. What do you think of this? If I said this, what would the kids at school say? How do you think most kids would feel if their dad said this to them? And so on. As we did this on various subjects, we were able to share our own opinions as well as learn from our kids.

I will confess that I hated to get into sticky or delicate subjects with my daughters. I guess I had the idea that innocence and virtue were connected to each other; if I could just keep my little girls sheltered from the ugliness of the world—from child molesters and flashers and other kinds of deviants—if they didn't know these things existed, then maybe they would go away. The sad truth is that in this world they are not going to go away. They are with us. They are a part of our culture. To send our daughters—or sons—out into this world without parental direction, without at least the understanding that we are aware of and willing to discuss what's going on out there, is to unnecessarily send them out as sheep among wolves.

When the Issue Is Divorce

In homes broken by divorce, teenagers need to discuss the breakup with their parents. I talk to many children of divorce who carry tremendous and unnecessary guilt because they feel something that they did contributed to the break up of the marriage. They may remember a parent losing his or her temper at them—and then soon leaving for good. Sometimes they think, *If they hadn't had such a difficult person as me to raise, maybe they wouldn't have been divorced.*

As difficult as it may be, sit down with a son or daughter after a divorce and relay your honest feeling—without putting the burden of responsibility on the estranged mate. The incompatibilities, the lack of unity, the dividing factors, need to be explained, though without putting the spouse down.

Many parents say, "But they wouldn't understand." Well, they have to live with the results of the split home, so they deserve at least a chance at trying to understand. If your children accuse you of self-centeredness — or carelessness or infidelity or shallowness — listen. Try to explain your own viewpoint, but let them work it through — deal with and struggle with — and understand how this most difficult of all family experiences happened. Kids moved off the solid rock of parental love by divorce deserve honest answers to honest questions.

Kenneth Chafin instructs us with these words:

> If more people understood what a divorce does to the persons going through it, they would react differently to people whose marriages fail. The best analogy I know is that divorce is like a death in the family. Instead of a physical death, it is the death of the deepest of all human relationships — marriage. All the pain and all the emotions present where physical death has taken place are involved. I have been with men and women at the time they lost their mate by death and have observed what this loss does to them physically and emotionally. I've sat with people after the death of a marriage and discovered almost identical reactions to this different kind of death.

> There is one sad difference between physical death and the death of a marriage. The family, the community, and the church know how to move in where someone has died and minister to those who grieve. When the time is near, the family and friends gather so one will not face the loss alone. After the death friends and neighbors come with words of concern, food for the table, and embracing arms.

> The visitation at the funeral home, the memorial service, and even the trip to the cemetery are a part of the way in which we have learned to comfort one another at the time of physical death. All these are done because we have come to know that at a time of great loss it is good for people not to be alone.

More than anything else, grieving people need to experience the love and concern of their friends and family.

But if the death is that of the marriage relationship, while the pain and grief may be just as real, the family and church and community have no plan of action to comfort and support these individuals. Usually, rather than helping, there is a drawing away because people do not seem to know what to do and say. So at a time when friends who love and care would be most welcome and needed they aren't there.

To complicate matters even further, in the death of a marriage there is no body to bury. The two persons go on living even though their relationship is dead and their presence is a constant reminder of the failure of the marriage. If there are children, though the marriage is over, the family goes on because there are still parents and children (the parents simply no longer live together).[4]

When the Issue Is Theology

Family questions can be very painful and so can theological questions. Not everything in the Bible is that easy to sort out or explain. Faith is not really an absence of doubt. Faith is maintaining confidence in God in the face of ambiguity, confusion, difficulty, and seeming injustices.

The wise parent does not assume a young person's questions indicate a lack of faith. When a big one is thrown on the table, you might say, "Yes, that's an interesting question that many Christians have thought about, including myself. Here is what I have concluded and why . . . ."

If your answer doesn't seem satisfactory, you might suggest that your son or daughter talk to the pastor or youth worker. Let that leader attempt to explain why he or she has come to certain conclusions. If several paths have been shared and the young person still isn't satisfied with answers, I suggest recommending a "suspended judgment." I usually say, "You know, I have hundreds of things stored away in my mind in suspended judgment. If I can't find an answer to them in this world, then as soon as I get with God, I'm going to ask Him. First Corinthians 13:12 says, 'Now we see through a glass, darkly; but then face to face.' I assume that in eternity the blinders will be taken off my eyes and I'll understand these things clearly." We sometimes need to acknowledge that all the answers aren't crystal clear to us mortals. Someday they will be.

I've Been There

I'm a strong believer in self-disclosure. A son needs to hear that a father has had his love spurned, that he's felt the heartache of being deemed unacceptable by a particular girl, that he's spent days thinking about little else but her. When a son knows that his father has felt this way, he knows he's not the only person in the world who has ever had this problem— which is probably how he's otherwise feeling.

Teens often feel totally alone in their struggles, embarrassments, and questions. Tomorrow may not be in the picture for them because all they see is today.

Bruce Narramore gives some good parental advice along these lines:

Deep feelings are changed with understanding and acceptance. If your adolescent is riding a tide of negative emotion, the best way you can help him to solid ground is to jump in with him. Let him know you're nearby, being ready to listen when he feels like talking. And be careful not to squelch communication by quick judgment or slick solutions. There are times for parents to give teens direct guidance, but in the middle of a strong emotion is not one of them. It is impossible to take in advice when one is full of negative emotions. It is like trying to spit and swallow at the same time! It can't be done. Not until some of the strong emotions have been dissipated are teens ready to take in any new perspectives.

At this point some Christian parents protest, "I know my teenager needs my understanding. But what if his emotions are wrong or sinful? The Bible says we should 'put away our anger' and 'the fruit of the Spirit is joy'—not depression. Shouldn't we help them see how these attitudes are wrong?"

Yes, you definitely should. But the problem is how to do it. Most of us are well aware that negative emotions should be resolved. And Christians know that certain attitudes are downright sinful. But even a sinful attitude cannot be changed immediately. Our attitudes, habits, and emotions are the product of years of experience and ingrained beliefs. To overcome them usually takes considerable time—along with a lot of understanding from a caring person. That is why we should never argue with a feeling.

No one has ever banished a deep feeling with an argument. Feelings change with time, understanding, and new perspectives. It is a process. When we allow our teenagers to express their pent-up emotions, they can gradually begin to see things in another light. Open exposure helps them see there are, indeed, "other fish in the pond" and that "the end of the world" hasn't arrived. But it takes time and tender, loving care.[5]

It helps to think of this world as being our Father's creation. The Devil cannot create anything; he can only hurt, bend, and twist. Everything in the world—including our sexuality, appetites, ambitions, desires, drives, fears—are given to us by God for various reasons. Learning to understand them is a part of our worship of God. Even though we don't know the answers, knowing that answers do exist can give us the confidence not to feel threatened by questions or insecurities evident in our teenagers. A calm, confident, humble, and faith-filled parent is a marvelous resource to questioning teenagers.

ELEVEN

FAILURE TO TAKE TIME

"I'm Kind of Busy Right Now.
Could You Come Back Later?"

Nearly every time I address parents of teens, someone asks, "Jay, don't you think the quality of the time you spend with your teenager is more important than the quantity?"

Even though I've been asked this question thousands of times, I try to be patient. I say, "I think I understand what you're trying to say, but there is no way to have quality time without having quantity time. No one is wise enough to know the best way to spend every minute. Our thinking is faulty when we say, 'I have five minutes free right now and I'm going to have some quality time with my daughter.' "

Have you ever sat down with a high school kid, looked her in the eye, and said, "I have an hour; let's communicate"? It doesn't work.

As I see it, spending time with a teenager is something like producing a documentary film. Over the years, I've helped produce a number of them for the Youth for Christ Ministry. We always attempted to produce first-class programs on a very low budget. With every movie came an unrealistic wish: if we could just go into this particular part of the city, or this foreign country, or this teenage hangout and somehow capture the spirit of the place in ten minutes. We'd save so much money that way. Film crews were expensive; film was expensive; time was expensive. But that's not reality. In reality, it worked like this: for every minute of the final film, we left approximately twenty hours of film on the cutting room floor. It takes a tremendous amount of raw material to produce one hard-hitting documentary. When you see an award-winning film, you can be sure that it cost hundreds of thousands, if not millions, of dollars. Why? Because it takes months to find the perfect shot that might come and go on the screen in three or four seconds.

And that's how it is with teenagers. You need to spend enough time with them to allow those wonderful, growing, teaching moments to happen.

Fortunately, every adult has experienced this in a friendship. A life-long friend once said to me, "Friendships have a way of turning a corner. You can be friends for quite a while before this happens. Then, maybe at an overnight retreat, maybe during a long trip together — it often happens when things go wrong — you end up with a block of unplanned time and that friendship turns a corner. You touch one another, reach one another, and, from that time on, you don't have to spend a lot of time in friendship maintenance; you don't have to spend a lot of time kindling the friendship every time you see each other. In two or three seconds, you're back on track; you're able to converse and communicate, and true friendship is there."

I am fortunate to have a number of people around the country with whom I have turned that corner. We've made commitments to each other that are lasting and true, and we'll never deny the other our presence if it's needed. I know at least two dozen men I could call if I needed them, who would be on their way to my side in a moment's notice — with no question as to what my need might be. They would come because we have established the kind of relationship that happens when people spend a quantity of time together sharing their souls.

This is the process that must take place in an adult's relationship with a teenager. If a father takes a boy on a hunting or fishing trip or to a basketball tournament or on a mountain-climbing expedition, that occasion is not about hunting or fishing or climbing mountains; it's about time spent together. It's about those twenty hours of "wasted" film on the floor of the cutting room that were necessary to get a three-second, power-packed scene. It's about the seemingly wasted time it takes to reach the moment when a boy says, "But Dad," and then begins to open up his soul.

There's no way around the fact that it takes time to get to know someone. Janie and I have lounge chairs in my study. We often sit in two corners of the room with our feet toward the center — not quite touching. I can hear her breathe. Her presence is comforting. Sometimes we spend an evening like this — each reading a different book, not speaking much, and yet communing with one another, feeling together and fulfilled. Our young people need to spend enough time with us for this to happen.

Being in a boat together, sewing a dress, overhauling an automobile engine, planting a garden, preparing for a competition, building a model — these parent-child activities in themselves are not as important as the time spent doing them.

I have a little rule: *Take a kid along.* If you're going to the drugstore or hardware, always ask one of the kids to go along. When you're driving, you can ask a question without making an ordeal out of it. Your daughter is looking straight ahead, just like you are. If she has an answer, she answers; if not, she says, "Look at that tree over there!" and changes the subject. You can talk to a son easier with your head under one side of a car hood and his under the other than you can if you are staring at each other. Some of the best conversations I've had with adolescents have been with casting rod in hand. It works like this. You cast and make a statement. Then your kid casts and makes a statement. After you spend a whole morning doing this, you'll look back on it and say, "Hey, we communicated."

There are, of course, ways to make any time together of greater quality. For instance, I've met people who are so preoccupied and unable to focus and listen that they make you feel as if you've not been heard.

A teenager once said to me, "I like our pastor."

"What do you like about your pastor?" I asked.

"Well, when you talk to him, you feel like you are there."

One of my favorite kids of all time said to me, "You know what I am?"

"What are you?" I asked.

"A comma," he answered.

When you meet a kid like this, listen, because he's got an important message. I said, "What do you mean, you're a comma?"

"Well, I'll be talking with my dad and he'll say something. Then when I start to talk, he pauses. He never interrupts me, but when I'm through he starts up again right where he left off. What I say doesn't really mean anything. I'm a comma."

Being a Christian bureaucrat, I meet presidents, senators, and the like, and I enjoy collecting pictures of them. (They always have a photographer there.) The pictures are hilarious — they show me shaking hands with all these famous people who are looking at somebody else! I'm only a reflection in their glazed eyes. An Australian wrote a book entitled *The Awesome Power of the Listening Ear,* and the title says it all.

Any parent who gives a young person his or her full attention is indeed giving more quality time than the one who is preoccupied.

I would encourage every parent to not think of themselves only in regard to function. Function-only parents think, *I provide housing. I provide clothing. I provide food. I provide some advice. What else could they need? They are warm. They are full. They are protected. They're warned, so what more is there?*

There is much more. There is what God has built into us — the desire to be with one another, to know one another, to care for one another. We were created as interdependent, social creatures.

The decision to spend time with your children is one of the most important ones you can make. And yet, spending time with your children often goes against our culture because business and industry make harsh demands.

Ultimately, every parent will be called to make choices. What is more important — a promotion that means we must move to another community or my daughter's senior year of high school? What is more important—working overtime or spending a Saturday with the kids? Years ago, while preparing a message to parents, I asked my children, who were then in elementary and junior high school, what activities they thought parents should do with their kids. They made a list, and I took it with me and read it to the parents. Surprisingly, almost none of the activities cost money. They listed activities like rake leaves together, go for a walk in the park, go to the zoo, make costumes for Halloween.

I previously mentioned one of my most respected family models, Don Lonie. The Lonies developed what they called family night. When the children were little, they invented a game called Sock, a version of tag played in the dark, in the house, in stocking feet. If you found somebody crawling on the floor, that person had to give you a sock. The person who ended up with a sock still on and who had collected the most other socks was the winner. Over the years, the Lonie's divided the family into teams. Sock was played every Thursday night, but about Monday they began to plan the game. Mom would say to the girls, "Hey, you be on my team on Thursday, okay? Let's beat the boys." They gradually developed sophisticated twists to the game. One person would flip the light switch off and on like a strobe light. The neighbors thought they were crazy. They heard screams, yelps, yips, and laughter; they saw lights flashing on and off; they wondered what kind of strange neighbors they had. When the kids were well into their teens, they still enjoyed an evening at home playing Sock with their family. Why? Because Sock was such an intricate and complex game? Not at all. They enjoyed it because Mom and Dad made the effort to spend time with them and gave them their full attention for an evening.

I believe that every hour spent with children will pay off later in their lives. When you spend quantity time, God rewards you with quality times, which will become the foundation of your future relationship. Almost every worthwhile question about life will eventually come up if a parent and child spend enough time together.

It's Only Half Time

I've discussed what I call the ten mistakes parents make with teenagers. Perhaps the title is a little threatening, as we've all made these mistakes — and many more. But the issues raised are central to the parenting process.

I have little patience with people who seem to believe that parents are destined to fail. As I see it, God would not have asked us to do something that we can't do.

The Bible is full of people, including parents, who faced challenges. Old Testament Jews lived in difficult times, among strange tribes with strange gods. Yet God told them to remain pure, to maintain their identity, to keep the truths God had given them, and to keep their Jewish identity before their young people. They were instructed to talk to their children about their relationship with God as they walked from place to place and as they sat at home. They were even to write it on doorposts. I don't believe these instructions are literal commands for this day, but they point out that we should always be conscious of our identity as God's people in the midst of a wicked and perverse generation.

New Testament Christians also faced difficult challenges. I've often wondered what it must have been like for a young, first-century Christian girl to work in a dining hall serving Roman soldiers. Imagine the ugly statements, the pinching, the slaps, the vulgarities. The people in the New Testament lived in a pagan society, a Roman culture with sexual perversions that would embarrass even twentieth-century film audiences. The people of God have always lived in a world that is not a friend of grace. But once again, I don't believe God would ask us to do something we can't do — raise our children to be sensitive to His Holy Spirit and to walk in His ways.

We dare not live like water coming down the side of a hill—seeking the path of least resistance. We must live with purpose and direction. We must understand who we are in contrast to the rest of the world. We must constantly stand guard—discussing, praying, talking, debating, forgiving, loving, waiting—using all the tools of grace as we lead our families. Families are not destined to failure. They can succeed. In fact, to the glory of God, I see more families with purpose and direction succeeding today than in years past.

Since coming to Taylor University, I've been encouraged by what I see on parents' weekend. With about fifteen hundred students on the campus, it's marvelous to watch parents spend a weekend with these post-adolescents. To see how many loving, caring families there are, how many dutiful, obedient young people there are, and to watch how much devotion and care they give one another is heartening to me. I sometimes wish that people who watch television and feel that the world is going to the dogs could see how many people are successfully, courageously, and victoriously living out the Biblical model of the Christian family. It is possible.

I've offered the ideas in this book with the prayer that they—along with other input and insights about the unique personality of your own family—will help you build positive relationships.

May you learn, as we have, that our relationship with our own children can be the most satisfying of all our relationships.

I've frequently said that Janie's relationship with our daughters is the closest she has with any women. The sound of their joy is music to my ears. They stand by the sink, sit at the kitchen table, and drink coffee and tea by the hour—giggling and laughing, simply enjoying one another. I know God smiles broadly as well.

Likewise, if I were to be parachuted into the frozen north or some tropical jungle and could choose only one man to be with, I'd choose my son. He is the most self-reliant, sensible, trustworthy man I could choose. There's no one to whom I would rather entrust my life, and I say this despite having lived with him through those tense years of adolescence. But now, at the end, I can say those years were worth the hassle.

Let me encourage parents: Don't count the score at half time. Don't believe that your children are going to freeze where they are now. They will grow. The same cause-and-effect lessons that you've learned, they too will learn. Some will learn from guidance and warnings, others will have to touch the stove to find out that it's hot. Some will go through deep pain, struggle, and agony. But the grace of God is working in their lives as it has in yours. And on the other side, they will come out as His children. Believe in process. Know that growth is taking place.

To those whose hearts are breaking in a time of estrangement, I want to say that some of these things, when viewed in the longer view of history, look like mere blips on the screen — momentary separations that, with time and prayer, will be healed by the grace of God.

God loves your family more than you do. Believe that the Holy Spirit is with your teenagers even when you are absent from them. The Holy Spirit is faithful. He is capable of breaking through the disharmony and noise of teenage life and of speaking in quiet places. The still small voice of God speaks today. And He speaks to sons and daughters.

Parenting is one of God's great ideas, and parenting teenagers is the best part of it. Just remember, mind your instincts; parent with confidence; consult His Word; pray much; then believe God for the reward.

END NOTES

Chapter 1

1. Gordon McLean, *What's a Parent to Do?* (Wheaton, Ill.: Victor Books, 1983), 14.
2. Bruce Narramore, *Adolescence Is Not an Illness* (Old Tappan, N.J.: Fleming H. Revell, 1980), 110.
3. Ibid., 36.
4. Paul Tournier, *A Place for You* (San Francisco: Harper & Row, 1968), 128.
5. Dolores Curran, *Traits of a Healthy Family* (Minneapolis: Winston Press, 1983), 23-24.

Chapter 2

1. McLean, *What's a Parent to Do?*, 92-93.

Chapter 3

1. David Seamands, *Healing for Damaged Emotions* (Wheaton: Victor Books, 1981), 29.
2. David Augsburger, *Caring Enough to Confront* (Glendale, CA: Regal Books, 1980), 13-15.

Chapter 4

1. Kenneth Chafin, *Is There a Family in the House?* (Waco, TX: Word Books, 1978), 124.
2. Mark P. Cosgrove, *The Amazing Body Human* (Grand Rapids: Baker Book House, 1987), 73-74.
3. Chafin, *Is There a Family?*, 127.
4. Anonymous, "Misgivings of a Christian Childhood," (n.p., n.d.).

Chapter 5

1. Josh McDowell, *What I Wish My Parents Knew about My Sexuality,* (San Bernardino, CA: Here's Life, 1987), 54-55.

Chapter 6

1. Donald Sloat, *The Dangers of Growing Up in a Christian Home* (Nashville: Thomas Nelson, 1986) 145-146.
2. Elizabeth Skoglund, *You Can Be Your Own Child's Counselor* (Glendale, CA: Regal Books, 1978), 21-22.
3. Charles R. Solomon, *The Rejection Syndrome* (Wheaton, Ill.: Tyndale House, 1982) 78-79.
4. Narramore, *Adolescence,* 67-68.

Chapter 7

1. McLean, *What's a Parent to Do?,* 48.

Chapter 8

1. Narramore, *Adolescence,* 92.
2. McDowell, *What I Wish,* 26.

Chapter 9

1. Paul Borthwick, *But You Don't Understand* (Nashville: Oliver-Nelson Books, 1986), 131-132.

Chapter 10

1. McDowell, *What I Wish,* 54-55.
2. Narramore, *Adolescence,* 24-25.
3. James Dobson, *Dare to Discipline* (New York: Bantam Books, 1970), 170-171,
4. Chafin, *Is There a Family?,* 139-140.
5. Narramore, *Adolescence,* 57-58.

COLOPHON

The typeface for the text of this book is *Baskerville*. Its creator, John Baskerville (1706-1775), broke with tradition to reflect in his type the rounder, yet more sharply cut lettering of eighteenth-century stone inscriptions and copy books. The type foreshadows modern design in such novel characteristics as the increase in contrast between thick and thin strokes and the shifting of stress from the diagonal to the vertical strokes. Realizing that this new style of letter would be most effective if cleanly printed on smooth paper with genuinely black ink, he built his own presses, developed a method of hot-pressing the printed sheet to a smooth, glossy finish, and experimented with special inks. However, Baskerville did not enter into general commercial use in England until 1923.

Substantive editing by Judith Markham
Cover design by Kent Puckett Associates, Atlanta, Georgia
Typography by Thoburn Press, Tyler, Texas
Printed and bound by Maple-Vail Book Manufacturing Group
Manchester, Pennsylvania
Cover Printing by Weber Graphics, Chicago, Illinois